RIO GRANDE WETBACKS

CARROL NORQUEST

Rio Grande
WETBACKS

~

MEXICAN
MIGRANT
WORKERS

UNIVERSITY OF NEW MEXICO PRESS · ALBUQUERQUE

FOR LEE

WHO FURNISHED THE ORIGINAL SPARK

CONTENTS

PREFACE

IN THE EARLY TWENTIES A SOUTH TEXAS land company reached its hungry tentacles into our peaceful Kansas county and carried off the cream of the county's farmers in railroad coaches. An excursion to the warm, lower Rio Grande Valley—Paradise, and all free! The temperature at home was nine below, and our gullible self-made rustics went readily. Later a shrewd relative of mine went back down to "La Gloria" and bought more land, this time on his own. He told me afterward, "I found out I'd paid the land company ten thousand dollars to locate me in the Valley, over and above the fair price of the land I bought from them—ten thousand dollars for a free trip!" He survived it, but a lot of people lost everything.

Neighbors who had relocated convinced my father that he should move to Texas and cure his rheumatism. They arranged a trade for him, his farm in Kansas for a piece of the bottomless alluvial soil of this flat, warm country, all less than 110 feet above sea level. The land was in the (by then defunct) W. E. Stewart Irrigation Company District, a district that was being reorganized by the landowners themselves: 32,000 acres, most of it covered with mesquite, *huisache*, ebony, *jara*, catsclaw, and nopal (prickly pear); infested with *javelinas*, deer, rattlesnakes, turkeys, descendants of longhorn cattle, and burros.

Incredibly, a town had been laid out in the center of the district—Edinburg, a fledgling community of five thousand.

Windmills of every design turned above the town, and wooden cisterns overhead showed through the foliage.

An old steam engine pushed our immigrant-car backward up the branch line from San Juan, piping her air whistle at animals on the tracks and stopping for us to chase off cows. Our former Kansas neighbors helped us unload. There was a large old house, dilapidated and paintless, on our land—a relic of the Stewart debacle. We fixed it up and lived in it. Father got over his rheumatism in the first year. When he and mother died, I inherited the old house and five acres.

The Depression came. Everyone was broke. The banks closed. I sold my last cotton crop—three little bales— for five cents a pound. After letting it stand idle for three years—without fuel to run it—I sold the tractor for junk. We paid $1.25 a day for help, if we had any money. That's what the government paid men to chop out the bermuda grass on public property, just to give them work. Sometimes people came by begging for work or food—dry corn, roasting ears, anything edible.

I went to McAllen every month or so, when I got lonesome, in my hen-specked, termite-eaten Model T Ford. I went to see a girl. I wasn't looking for a wife. I was too poor, and I was afraid of girls anyway. Still, she never acted ashamed of my rusty jalopy standing in front of her house. Finally I told her I'd let her come out and cook for me if she'd fill that big old house with kids, but that the Lord would have to fulfill His promises and provide the stuff to cook, because I sure as hell didn't have enough sense to. She came and He did. Our seven kids were all born and raised here. She lacked one of filling the house, but I got a good deal, I think, for she's gotten prettier every year as her hair gets grayer. Her name was Lydia. We found out that it was also a good Spanish name; our Mexican friends always called her "Lee-dee-ah."

World War II came and money began to trickle. Edinburg

had no packing plants then, only a stockyard. Wages went to thirty cents an hour, although most farm work was done by contract: so much a package, row, and so on.

The wetbacks began to come in droves: *mojados*, Mexicans in this country illegally, who had crossed the Rio Grande to work. They were everywhere in those days, men, women, and children. Babies were born in their camps over the district, in brush patches, on canal banks. Their dead were buried in country cemeteries. The climate here is favorable for camping, especially for people who were used to nothing better—semi-arid, with little cold weather and very little rain most of the year. Any farmer who was known to have work was swamped with help.

Businesses grew through the years. Four mammoth tomato packing plants went up. Trainloads of tomatoes went north at night. Citrus groves were put in and five citrus plants came, seven cotton gins, three tomato canning plants. The country was cleared of the brush that had been full of wetback camps. Road rights-of-way were cleared, roads graded, later some paved. Mail routes, telephones, electricity, and now pressured water came.

My biggest farm operation was 400 acres, 120 of which were my own. Some years I had 250 bales of cotton, but most years it was under a hundred bales. Some sold for thirty-six cents a pound. As the economy picked up from nothing, I could buy tractors for power; the last one I bought cost $1,500.

Then under government controls costs doubled and redoubled. A similar tractor now costs $6,000 or $7,000, and repair bills are proportionately higher. Many of our young operators have gone to Mexico for cheaper labor and supplies and freedom from controls. Trainloads of tomatoes, peppers, and other produce come across our railway bridges. Five wide automobile bridges span the Rio Grande. U.S. brokers go to Mexico to buy fruit, pack it, and ship it back to our former markets, hauling by truck or railroad right through our once-productive farms.

Farmers here can't make a living. Most have quit. We have no tomato sheds or canning plants, and only two part-time gins. Commodity prices are lower than when we had large production. The big operators are trying their wider wings here in the Valley, but they'll be forced out too.

Plenty of wetbacks are still coming across, in spite of three sets of Mexican police that patrol the river, and a large body of our own border patrol. But the laborers are going more and more into migrancy.

These stories are about the Mexican wetbacks I've known and worked with over the years. The stories are true, as far as I was given the ability to write the truth. Some are tales that were told to me by neighbors, some of which I've included to illustrate areas of activity that my being tied down to the farm didn't allow for. The people in them are real, though many are now dead. No character is invented.

All names have been changed. I think they would have been happy for me to use their names, but I could not know who an exception might be. It was hard for me to substitute fictitious names for my friends in writing about them. Their real names are the real story. Some may recognize themselves. If so, I will be honored; I will have written true.

The dialogue in most cases is a direct translation from *el idioma de la frontera*—the Tex-Mex of the border. *La chota*, for example, is colloquial for the U.S. border patrol. I did not translate conversations into idiomatic English; if I had, this would be an English story, out of place.

For help with this book, I thank Professor Harry Quin at Pan American University for the incentive he gave me; also my friends Bruno Lopez and Ruben Zamora, who were pleasantly available for Tex-Mex consultation at all times. And to the many friends who gave me episodes that were not included here, I say that their stories were not omitted for lack of worth but only because of space limitations. The other stories will be preserved for later use.

In some cases, wetbacks were treated as trash. The people in these sketches are my friends, and it hurt me when I saw them taken advantage of. If I ever was guilty of mistreating them, I'm not aware of it; none of them has ever said so. The worst offenders, I found, were often of their own blood—labor contractors, overseers, bosses—Mexicans whose families had come to the United States a generation or more before, whose standards of living and education had risen. Some greedy Mexican *jefes* on this side of the border earned a name for their imperious treatment of the wetback, their cousin from across the river. It is an onus that the whole agricultural community has to bear in the eyes of the press and labor unions. But most wetbacks did not lose anything by coming, no more than did the earlier immigrants to the United States from Europe or Asia or Africa.

I present the people here without furbishing. They are human beings, with all the faults and good things of all peoples. They have the feelings, souls, ambitions, envies, kindnesses, and plain meannesses of all of us.

As has been true everywhere else, it is not the wealthy who will finally settle the Valley. It is the poor, who furnish the sweat and muscle and kids, whose descendants will be its inhabitants. The big shots will disappear into anonymity—leave or peter out. The poor will inherit its space.

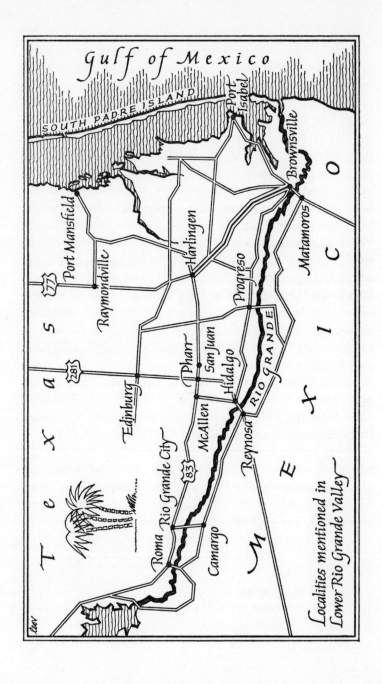

Localities mentioned in
Lower Rio Grande Valley

INTRODUCTION

PEEWEE WAS BARKING SAVAGELY, TELL-ing us a Mexican was in the yard somewhere. I finished breakfast before I stepped out.

The screen door slammed disjointedly behind me. I rounded the corner of the house on the patio, feeling expansive, full of pancakes and bacon. I gave the long barn and machine shed a swift glance, and from the corner of my eye caught a head quickly withdrawn into the uncertain, early-morning shadows behind the car.

I ambled indirectly toward it, tossing a stick at Peewee's insistent racket, and reached the shed entrance behind the car. The shadow stepped out, carrying a dirty straw hat, and bowed slightly.

"Buenos días, señor."

"Buenos días," I returned noncommitally.

He advanced, glanced up and down the road. Then, "No tienes trabajo, señor?"

It might have been "No tienes chamba?" or "No gottee workee?"—depending on where in Mexico he came from.

The time was the early forties. Mexico, unlike us, was not at war. She had an overabundance of strong, healthy, young men and women. They were very poor, in deep poverty even by Mexican standards.

They would come up to my farm early in the morning and stop a little distance from the house, off Peewee's property range, showing themselves only after I appeared.

Our agricultural community was drained of young men. Those not cleaned out by the draft were up at Corpus Christi working on the expanding naval air base, or farther north on some other succulent government project, their families with them. Our government economists were calling for more food, more fiber, but we did not have the labor to operate our farms. Farmers' sons were gone, too.

The people across the Rio Grande knew these things, clear down to Campeche and Yucatán, through some grapevine of the illiterate. Like locusts they came, daring long miles to the river, to cross an expanse of turbulent water pushing their skimpy clothing ahead on a piece of driftwood. No one knew where they would alight. The Tamaulipas police were inadequate, our border patrol too thin. We farmers were willfully unable to ascertain whether the new workers were "wet" or not, so we hired them. The burden of proof was on the local authorities, and they were swamped by the numbers of newcomers.

I made a show of finding out something about the new man.

"Where from are you?"

"From San Luis Potosí." It might just as well have been Guanajuato or Durango or Floresville, Texas. Quite often their answers were true.

"Yes, I have work. What can you do?"

"I can do anything you might have for me. Hoe, shovel—tractor, no."

"Can you irrigate?"

"Sí, señor."

"I could use you, but I have no place—no little house, no room."

"There's no difference—under those oranges," pointing, "or in that little old house," an old chicken house on the other side of the barnyard. "Or have you some old boards, a piece of canvas? It makes me no difference—I'll stay over there," he waved his arm vaguely in a wide arc, "anywhere."

"How much money do you want?"

"Whatever you can pay. But, por favor, do you have a little for me to eat? I have much hunger. No have I food since day before yesterday."

I saw that he was really hungry. "Who may know? I will ask mi madama what she has."

So I made arrangements with Lee for a couple of egg sandwiches or the leftover pancakes. This was standard practice at our home, whether a man went to work or not. But this one was really hungry, not a freeloader.

While he ate, trying not to wolf his food, I asked when he had crossed the river.

"Last night," he replied.

"And you have come all this way since the sun went down, by foot?"

"Sí, señor."

"You must have traveled fast."

"Sí, señor. I wanted to leave many miles behind me."

"Then you must be very tired."

"No, señor," he laughed, "I'm not tired. I'm used to the walk on foot. I live on the mountains. In what kind of work do you want me?"

The arrival of my regular hands in the barnyard for work disconcerted him a little. They were sizing him up, too.

"You want some food from town, some provisiones?"

"Sí, señor, por favor. I need a little food, not much. Saturday, I you pay."

"Have you a family?"

"Sí, señor," proudly, "I have a woman and four chamacos. There they all stayed with the mother of mi esposa."

And so I'd hired an alien. I'd committed a crime—the first

of many to come, piled on top of each other. But he was hungry; I had work for him. His family needed money; I had the money. He'd be a loyal worker and a loyal friend. He wouldn't gallivant. All he'd ask would be to work and to be left alone.

For the moment, he'd tell me what he wanted from town: clothes, their quality and size, cooking utensils to set himself up in housekeeping, food. He wanted badly to stay out of town.

In a few months he'd go home with his money, maybe asking me to pick him up somewhere along the river when he returned. Or he might have an address to which I could send a money order, so he couldn't be robbed on the way. Or he might send the money with a friend who was homeward bound.

Later, as he became more familiar with the work and my managing, he would go home and stay for days, weeks, months, even a year. Then some morning he'd be standing in the barnyard again with Peewee barking at him, ready to go to work. But first he'd have to tell me all the news of his family.

He might have had a spat with his woman. Maybe another man had moved in; maybe she had left. Maybe he had a new woman, had brought her with him and hidden her somewhere along a fence line or canal until he could break the news to me; a younger one who would be happy to share his established camp, cook for him, stay hidden from *la chota*, the border patrol.

His trust in *el patrón*, if his patron was good to him, was complete. Life, liberty, health, welfare, money—he put them all in the hands of el patrón. He gave in return the very best that was in him: good wishes, regard, loyalty, ,and labor.

We needed these people; our country needed them. Our country needed our produce; their country needed their cash. The laws would not allow us to use them honestly, so we all— wetbacks, farmers, lawmen, even la chota—became liars. Everybody made a flimsy show of being law-abiding; that was all.

When the wetback went back to his country to stay, he was a trained agriculturalist. He could service and drive a tractor. He could plant seed and adjust cultivators. His country needed his kind, and later it made determined efforts to keep them at home.

He had a higher standard of living than before. He had observed. His simple wants had increased; he liked ice cream and Coca Cola, Stetson hats, and real shoes. He could use a can opener. His wants now had to be met in his own country.

He had, in a sense, been going to school—a practical one—and he had been paid for going. He was educated.

All illegal.

CHAPTER ONE

The
Families

MANY WETBACKS, ESPECIALLY IN LATER years, became migrant workers in this country, following the crops and the seasons north, east, and west. For the most part, they remained anonymous transients, and much has been written about the abuses against them and their suffering.

In the Valley many wetbacks came back again and again, year after year, to the same employers. The groups changed with the years, but in many cases we knew whole families—brothers and sisters, husbands and wives, uncles and cousins. We visited their homes in Mexico and met fathers, grandfathers, great-grandfathers. We saw their children grow up; some of them were born on our farms, and, U.S.–born, were U.S. citizens.

The stories in this chapter are about some of these people.

The Errand Boy

THE FAMILIA DE LEÓN WAS BASED around Quatro Palmas, a scattered little community on the road to Nuevo Laredo. There were seven brothers and three sisters, all grown, in the immediate family pertinent to these stories. It was an ancient river family of which the *primos*

7

(cousins) numbered into the hundreds to the third and fourth generations.

Some claimed to be American, some were definitely Mexican, but a large part of the family didn't know which they were and cared less. They were equally at home on either side of the Rio Grande. They were all expert swimmers who could hold their clothes out of the water in one hand or put them on a piece of driftwood and come across like beavers.

Trinidad was the youngest of the ten, and a man apart in his family, the only one who had a *bautismo* certificate, proof of U.S. citizenship. He had been born in Mercedes, Texas, a border town, when his mother was there one time "wet"—on a visit, or maybe deliberately to foal a U.S. citizen. Like the rest of his family, Trinidad knew no English. He had been raised in Mexico.

Trini received some schooling, but he didn't absorb much, for he was slow. "Mentally retarded," they say now. "*Tonto*" or "*sonso*," the Mexicans called him.

When I'd say something to him, he'd quickly turn to someone, preferably a brother, and ask, "What said Carlos? Eh? What said Carlos?" He did the same with his friends, so I knew it was not because of my ill-spoken Spanish. Anything said to him had to be confirmed by someone else close to him.

Trini was always showing up at odd times and patiently waiting for my attention. He never saw any need to hurry. He never got excited unless one of his brothers was riding him; then sometimes he would answer back sharply. He was single-minded and hung onto a thought until it was jarred loose by someone forcing another on him. But he had status in the community: He was American. No one would let you forget that. He had proof.

He understood no work except picking cotton. Then he led the crew and did good, clean picking. Hoeing required thought, deciding where to strike. It tangled him up.

His family used him as an errand boy. He could understand directions; he knew his way from here to there if he'd been over the ground once. When someone at Quatro Palmas needed money from a family member working on this side of the river or had a message to deliver, their first thought was of Trini. He could pass back and forth at will with his *papel de bautismo*. They would give him bus fare and toll money for the bridge; Trini would put on a clean white shirt and brown shoes, and over he'd come.

Once he tried to go north to work in Indiana with a truckload of wetbacks. The highway patrol upstate stopped them and confiscated Trini's papers, a calamity, bundled him together with the wetbacks, and sent him back to Mexico by airplane—all the way to Tampico. Trini finally filtered back up to the border, across the river, and on to my home. Prompted by eager siblings, he sputtered out his tale of woe.

"Sin vergüenza!" Without shame! "La chota stealing my papers! Me an American! Sending me like a chicken to Tampico! What can be done, Carlos? Where can I see the policía?"

"But Trini, amigo, how can you prove to anybody that you are an American? You speak no English. You look like a Mexican, your clothes are Mexican, you act like a Mexican. How am I to prove that you are an American?"

"But you, Carlos, can go to the police, or to la chota. Tell them I'm American! They will believe you. You're a man muy importante. Everybody knows Don Carlos."

I laughed. "Thank you, Trini, but this is not Mexico. They can't take money in the hand here. If I went with you to these officials of whom you think, they'd laugh at me and at you too. They'd bundle you right up and dump you back into Mexico. Maybe put you in jail—in el tanque."

"Yes, Carlos, I know, but there is something that might be done, no?"

"Yes, I think so, but it will need time. Patience. It is better that you don't get caught again. Stay on the other side of the river and we will think up a plan. You must have papers when you wander around in the United States. And when you have new papers, it will be better if you stay here in the Valley, and not go with mojados trying to sneak north. All the papers in Texas won't serve you if you herd with those wetbacks."

"Sí, Carlos, I understand all that, but I'm an American. I was born here. Soy Americano!" he shouted.

We were getting nowhere. I fell back on giving him simple orders.

"Trinidad, go you and ask your mamá where you were baptized in Mercedes, by whom, and every other thing she can remember. Have your sister Aurelia put it down on a piece of paper, and you bring the paper to me. Do you understand, Trini?"

He smiled his slow toothy smile. "I will do that, Don Carlos. Soy Americano."

El Tanque

"TORÍBIO DIDN'T COME TODAY," RAFAEL de León informed me with his crooked grin one Monday morning.

"When will he come?" I asked.

"That only knows God. En el tanque is he again. Also his friend of business, Coko."

"Yes? Why are Tor and his friend Coko in jail? Mojados?"

"Sí. They were going to carry a cargo of mojados across the river in the big boat when the Tamaulipas police caught them."

"Where are they?"

"Sabe Diós." God knows. "I think they are in Reynosa."

I heard no more about Tor and his friend Coko for a couple
of months. Then I found Trinidad waiting in the shade of
the mesquite in the yard. He told me that Tor wanted to see
me.

"Where is Tor now, Trini?"

"In el tanque yet, same as last week and the week before."

"In what town?"

"In Reynosa."

"For what does he want to see me?"

"Me, he did not tell. But he told me to say, 'There is no
hurry.' "

So I would have to pay another visit to that stinking jail!
The place reeked of stale urine. For Tor and many of the
others, I guess, the stay in jail was like a vacation. Bed and
food, free from worry. Tor certainly wasn't concerned about
his reputation; he didn't know he had anything called a
reputation to lose. All he had was that mouthful of gold teeth
that he showed when he grinned. That would be the first
thing I'd see through the bars—gold teeth!

But when I did see him, after entering the high, unguarded
gate of the building, he was not behind bars. He was strolling
along the north side of the wide, tiled corridor, a new straw
sombrero cocked on the side of his head. It struck me as
strutting, but it wasn't on my account, for I watched him before he saw me. Then he greeted me publicly from a distance
in his high, cackling voice, all the gold teeth showing.

"Ah qué Carlos! I'm happy to see you. What brings Don
Carlos to the carcel?" I joined him and we shook hands.

"To see my compadre Toríbio, porqué no? What are you
doing here, Tor?"

"Ah, Carlos amigo, how sad it is that they caught me. Just
as I had a full load in the big boat. Those river policía, they
sneak around in the dark! Carlos, I'm going to quit carrying
the people to the other side."

"Oh? Are you thinking strongly of dying, then, Tor?"

"Well, who knows, Carlos? But then, I'm having a good time here. Plenty of food, no work."

"Here, Tor. Here are some cigaros I brought you. But I thought you would be well closed in, like the other times."

"They know me here, Carlos. They know they can trust me. I help. I'm a jailer."

I laughed. It was totally improbable. "Eh, Toríbio, what makes you think you're a jailer? What nonsense have they been putting into your head?"

"No, Carlos," he replied earnestly, "you think I jest. See that room," pointing, "with the woman's arm hanging out? That room, I have charge of. See, I have the key on my belt."

"What do you have in there, a woman?"

"No, Carlos," eyeing me sideways. "There are twelve."

"Twelve women? Toríbio, you jest!"

"No, Carlos, it's the truth. Come and see."

I backed down quickly. "No, Tor, I don't want to see. But why are they there?"

"Some are thieves, some bad women, putas. One tried to kill her man. I don't know all."

"What do you do with them, Tor?"

"My business is to see they don't fight, and things like that."

"You're really advancing in the world, Tor! But not yet have you told me what you want of me."

"I want something of you, Carlos?"

"Yes, Trini came to my house and told me that you wished to see me but that you were not hurried."

"Oh, that! That was a long time pasado. No, Carlos, it all goes well with me now. I have some dinero—unos dolares. I'm paid a little, in the hand behind the back, and the work is not hard. God knows how much time it will be necessary for me to stay here. But I don't think it will be long.

"But they don't pay me much, it's true. I don't cost them

much as a jailer. Maybe they will keep me here for that reason."

I Buy a Cotton Picker

EACH YEAR I TOLD MY PICKERS WHEN they left for home after the cotton picking season, "God only knows, but to me it seems that this is the last year you people will pick for me. La chota is going to be bigger, going to sweep all of you mojados back to Mexico."

They'd listen gravely, but the next year here they'd come again—and my cotton would get picked.

In town one day in the middle forties, I was idly looking at the implement company's warehouse full of glistening, freshly painted machinery—wondering how we farmers could possibly be expected to buy all the new implements. Mr. Rake, the manager, came over.

"Mr. Rake, when are you going to get a cotton picker down here to show us?" I asked. "I've read in the papers, the last couple of years, that they're hot stuff."

"All the allotments have been going to California," he replied, "but I have the promise of three for next season's delivery, for sure."

"Do they really work?"

"You bet your life they work. I saw one working out in New Mexico last year. Do you want one?"

"I'll need one if they ever stop the wetbacks, and they're making a lot of noise about it this year. Say it's the real thing, they're going to sew the border up tight."

"That's right, it looks like it. California and Arizona haven't had as many wetbacks as we have here; that's why the company has been allotting all the pickers to them."

"Well, I want to speak for one now, but I'd like to see one working."

"All right, Mr. Norquest. In June, as soon as there's enough open cotton, there'll be one working on an experimental basis down south of Pharr."

All of our lives we'd heard that cotton would always defy machine picking. Now I had seen a machine pick it. The results were of lower quality than hand picking, but that was to be expected.

I hated to spend eleven thousand dollars on a machine to put on my big tractor, but apparently I had no choice. I signed a contract. The year rolled around, and my picker came in. It wasn't ready for delivery; they said it needed a lot of adjusting, and they had to train men to service it.

My cotton was opening and here came my old pickers, drifting in, one or two a day—members of the de León family, their neighbors, others. They clamored to start picking. I bought them some sacks, moved a trailer to the field, and let them pick. They had to eat.

Then the machine was ready. The cotton kept opening, but the hands kept coming and kept it picked. I was in a dilemma.

"No can la chota stop you people? I've bought me a machine to pick my cotton!"

"We have not seen la chota, Don Carlos."

"I thought I told you not to come this year."

"But we are here, Carlos. We need a little work. No pick we much."

The agent kept asking me, "When do you want that picker delivered?"

"I don't know, Mr. Rake," I said. "I don't want to bring a machine out unless I have enough cotton open to justify it. But my hands are picking the cotton as fast as it opens. I can't run them back home. The border patrol and the press were just full of hot air about eliminating the wetbacks for good; they fooled me again."

My cotton was half picked and my pickers hadn't been raided even once. Where was la chota? The men razzed me about the machine.

"When is the picker of the tractor coming, Carlos? We desire much to see it pick the cotton!"

Mr. Rake didn't push me, but I was getting more and more worried about his needing to fulfill the contract and deliver. I didn't want to take on that big debt for nothing. At last I went to him with my hat in my hand.

"Mr. Rake, I don't see how I'm going to need that picker this year. My cotton is over half picked already."

"Well, Mr. Norquest. The company is howling for that picker. They want it out in California; their cotton is just now getting ready to pick. We'll load it on a truck and send it out there."

So that was my cotton picker experiment.

The wetback problem eased up after the introduction of the *bracero* program—legal entry to work. The government cotton program limited our acreage. Custom picking by machines from Mississippi became widespread in the Valley.

Cotton pickers improved. I was fortunate that I hadn't been stuck with one of the early models.

Going Home

ONE LATE-SUMMER EVENING MY OLDEST sons, Rikki and Kelly, and I sat on a drift log on a mud-covered spit along the north bank of the Rio Grande. The brown water flowed swiftly past us into a stiff Gulf breeze from the southeast that ruffled the surface of the river. Deep silt deposited on the spit had dried, forming a checkerboard of curled blocks that crackled under our feet.

"How deep do you think it is, Daddy?" asked Rikki, thoughtfully studying the muddy water.

"I'd guess thirty, maybe forty feet," I answered, wondering if anyone knew. "Why?"

"Tor, Andrés, and the others swim around in there, they say."

"Yes, but they've lived beside it all their lives."

Kelly got up and tried to throw a hunk of crusted mud across. It didn't go far.

"It must take a lot of nerve for them to come across all that water—and risk being picked up by the border patrol," he commented.

I agreed. "A lot of people have drowned. Tor, Rafael, and the others don't show up to work much anymore because they're ferrying wetbacks across in their boat. They make more money that way."

"Yes, but," Kelly insisted, "I wouldn't cross that river just to work."

"You would if you got hungry enough," I told him, "and it would be hard for anyone to stop you. Look at these men standing here with their picking sacks full of stuff they've bought to take home; I've never asked any of them to come over and work."

Rikki laughed. "They always show up at cotton picking time. Not even la chota can keep them away."

"Right. That cotton picker I bought this year, thinking the border patrol was going to keep out the men! There are just too many of them. We have the work and the money to pay. Their police can't keep them home and ours can't keep them out. Their wives and kids need the things in those sacks—can you imagine how they'll be welcomed home?"

The men had gathered behind us, lounging quietly by their laden sacks and peering across the river. They were waiting patiently, sometimes with a low murmur, for *la lancha*—the boat.

They had finished picking my cotton, had been paid, had traded part of their money for goods in town. They had stuffed their purchases in their worn picking sacks and loaded them all in a cotton trailer that afternoon. With the trailer in tow behind the pickup, we'd left for the river.

We came the half-mile through the brush to the water single file, on foot. Flop-eared Gerónimo took the point, walking fast, and slid down onto the spit first. At once he put down his heavy burden and whistled shrilly, aiming his whistle at an old, white stucco, flat-roofed settlement a half-mile across the river. Slender-legged Antonio followed swiftly, stuck two fingers in his mouth, and added his own piercing whistle to his uncle's. It was a prearranged signal for someone to come over after them. The other men kept sliding down the bank and gathered around.

The wait seemed interminable. Finally sharp-eyed Jesús-María (who knew just where to look) exclaimed, "Allí vienen!" The crowd stirred and murmured. Standing up, I caught a glimpse of movement by a mesquite tree on the other side.

Two small figures came quickly down the bank, slid the boat into the water, and began to paddle energetically. They disappeared around some jara, going upstream, hugging the bank. We caught glimpses of them only when they hit a patch of sunlight in the shadows.

"Why are they going that way?" Kelly was disturbed by the delay. "That's away from us!"

"They're going upstream to gain momentum. When they've

gone far enough, they'll turn and come slanting across the current toward us, fast. They're paddling upstream over there where there isn't much current—in the eddies," I explained.

Silence descended on the group, broken only by the noisy cicadas sawing away in the thorny huisaches on the bank. Then, "Allí vienen," Alfonso repeated quietly. "Sí," agreed several of the others as they stretched their necks and squinted into the afternoon sun shimmering on the water.

La lancha came bobbing swiftly on the water like a doodlebug hanging onto a bit of bark. Tor, gold-toothed and grinning in the bow, paddled occasionally; Ernesto, bare-headed in the stern, guided.

What a boat! Two horizontal two-by-fours fastened together by two pieces of corrugated iron roofing, which bellied down between them and were caulked together with *chapapote*—asphalt—to keep out the water. The two-by-fours extended fore and aft, serving as handles for carrying the boat. The hand-carved, square-bladed paddles with mesquite-wood handles looked tremendously awkward.

Toríbio and Ernesto beached the boat quickly on the shallow spit and jumped out. After the *abrazos* and *saludos*—huggings and greetings—Tor turned to Ernesto.

"Don't slacken. Load la lancha. We have many voyages this night to make."

Carefully, Hector Tovar placed his long picking sack amidships, balanced it, and put his son Emilio's sack behind it.

"Compadre," I told Hector quietly, "it is very heavy for the lanchita, with all of these things and you and Emilio too. I'm afraid for you."

Hector, with the load balanced to his satisfaction, was unconcerned. His broad swarthy face lighted up with a smile that spread his wiry black mustache, fanlike.

"It is not necessary to fear for us." He pulled his new white Stetson down tighter and glanced at his half-grown son Emilio, who was visibly happy to be going home. "Go with God," he added as he offered his hand to the boys and me. "Many, many thanks and many salutations to your woman and the rest of your children."

Ernesto, uneasily steadying the boat, urged Emilio, "Mount yourself!" In one bound Emilio straddled the sack in the middle. Ernesto jumped into the bow. From the spit Hector lined up the boat for the other side, leaped astraddle the stern sack, and started to paddle furiously. Ernesto in front took up the stroke, and off they went, bouncing over the wavelets, tacking down river for Mexico and home.

I let out my breath, only then realizing that I'd been holding it—expecting that lacy craft to fold or roll over or just sink. I turned to Tor.

"How much time will you spend in carrying all across? There are twenty-nine more."

He glanced quickly over the crowd and their sacks. "Nearing the middle of the night."

To cross that company of men and their cargoes in that frail canoe yet tonight! I didn't see how the boat could float even the first cargo over the expanse of rough water.

"Won't it be very dark?" I asked.

"Yes, but I have the eyes like a cat and Ernesto too knows the river, and Rafael, and Antonio. There is no difference how obscure it gets."

"I thought you had many boats, Tor." He regularly swam out into the river rises and salvaged straying boats.

"Yes, I did," he laughed, "but la policía from me they confiscated all and almost carried me, too, to el tanque. I promised to them that I would never own another boat to carry mojados to los Estados Unidos."

"Yes, but you've got that wondrous thing," I pointed to the receding lancha, now nearing midcurrent. "It's a thing of much beauty," I teased.

"That no lancha is," he answered, grinning. "That is a trough for the oxen. We throw corn fodder into it for the beasts. When come to our house the police, they find no boat, they say to me, 'Muy bueno, Toríbio, as long as you have no boat, we are your friends.' And when comes a poor one who can't swim, we pick up our trough and trot to the river. When he returns with the money from his work, he pays me. I have no fear."

I laughed. He added, "I cannot help it if the trough for the oxen is fit to take the poor one to the other side."

"Indeed, Tor, it is a trough more handsome than it is a boat, but take care that they don't carry you to el tanque. I don't wish to come to el tanque again."

"Care for myself? I will be sure, but they are friends of mine and will not see a trough for the oxen—if I pass into the hand a little sweetening." He held up his hand and rubbed his thumb with his forefinger. Everyone laughed.

The sun was going down behind the trees on the other side of the river. The boys and I had to leave. I turned to the other men to say goodbye.

"Another year I'll come, if la chota does not catch me," said Nicolás in farewell.

"Who knows?" I answered. "If there is good cotton and if God so wishes, another year, yes. But one year soon, you can't. Too many la chota, too dangerous for a poor one." I kept shaking hands. "When the war stops itself, soldiers will come home and they will want to work. We will not need you mojados; we will have less need for good crops. Then we will see you, our friends, no more."

"God grant that it will not be so," they said.

Sweetening Land

IT TROUBLED ME TO EMPLOY THE MEN
steadily for two months, then send them away. During this time
they earned good money to send home, but they and I knew
that the end of each year's picking season was the end of
their good earnings for another year. They went home to whatever economic fate awaited them. Miguel caught me alone
one day and asked, "Is there no manner, Don Carlos, that
you can keep me employed? No more work of any kind?"

"Not unless I could employ you to make improvements, to
repair. But you are not a carpenter, or cement worker, or
plumber. What can you do?" There didn't seem to be any
satisfactory answer.

Luis made the same plea at the water can another time. I
asked him the same question. "Anything, Carlos, if you me
show!" he answered. The others, too, sidled up at odd times.
"Can you not find something for us to do?" "Just show us,
and we will do it."

You might as well do it yourself as stand and show someone else, I'd think. But my thoughts kept coming back to it,
trying to find something profitable for them and practical for
me.

My home place—the forty acres we had settled on when we
first came to Texas—had become too salty to farm, from river
water dumped on it year after year (eons, geologically), from
seepage out of irrigation company earthen canals, and from
over-irrigation. Seed would not sprout in the soil. I had
abandoned it for planting and let cattle range on it.

The alluvial delta of this dry country, brought down from
the even drier mountains of northern Mexico, west Texas, and
New Mexico, is full of soluble salts and alkalies. The soil has
never been leached by rains. You can taste the minerals in the

soil and its waters, see them white on top of the ground. The saturation goes deep, twenty-five feet and more.

Water travels laterally through this extremely porous subsoil, surfaces again at a distance, and evaporates. All of the solubles it contains originally, plus those it picks up in going through the salty subsoil, are left on top of the soil in crystal form where the water evaporates, and kill all vegetation except mesquite trees.

I believed that if I could reverse this process—irrigate with comparatively sweet water and let it carry the solubles with it into a drain line, thence to a discharge—I could sweeten the topsoil again. Not completely, but enough so that plant life would grow. I decided to do this some time when I could finance it; it would be costly in money and labor. I explained it to the men.

"Oyes, how would it go with you if I bought cement pipes to bury in the ground, to carry off this water to the drainage ditch? Can you bury them?"

They were eager. "Cómo no!" exclaimed Ernesto. "If the patron will us show! How much time will it last, the work?"

"Knows only God. If it costs me the same with you as it would bring a big machine to do the job, who knows? Maybe three, maybe six months."

"Just show us, Carlos," Hector assured me. "If it is not successful, we will stop work and return to Mexico."

So I borrowed a transit, measured, staked, ran grades. I bought fifteen shovels and welded a foot-rest on each. We broke ground. I contracted the men as braceros, so that they had papers and could come and go as they pleased. We spent the winter tiling. I was not happy; the work seemed to drag. I worried with them, and about what it was costing me.

It was instructive, though. Day after day the men dug ditches from seven to nine feet deep in the quaking alluvial soil of the Valley. The sides of the trenches were smoothed by the sharp shovels. They lay open for days. I would study them; stop and look, then drop down into a trench and inspect it.

How the Rio Grande could deposit the soil in different colors, in countless intricate patterns and irregular designs, horizontal and perpendicular, is a mystery to me. How can water deposit a thin column of fine sand in a solid expanse of granite? A crooked vein of black material in an expanse of orange or red? How can a washbasin-like area be formed of impervious material deep in the ground—and be water-logged while the surrounding area stays bone dry?

The men would stop work, too, to examine and wonder. They carved niches in the smooth trench side and stood in them little statues they had formed from the sticky yellow and red subsoil.

It was not until we finished, six months later, that my figures showed that the tiling job had cost me practically the same as if a big contractor had done it.

After the tile was laid and everything covered again, we watched the clear, sparkling water trickle from the outlets of the tile lines. It tasted as if all the chemicals of a drugstore had been dissolved in it. I left the end of one of the lines exposed for observation, and after ten years of irrigating and rainfall this steady trickle of drain water was as foul-tasting as at first.

The experiment worked. The solubles in the topsoil leached downward and out, countless tons of them in those steady little streams. It left the topsoil sweet. Anything will grow there now.

Wetbacks at Home

THE NEIGHBORHOOD AT QUATRO PALMAS had changed in the two years since I had last seen it. There was more greenery, but it looked more desolate for all that. I tried to fix the difference, but it eluded me.

The thatched houses placed helter-skelter and the white stucco store looked the same. I drove up on the west side and stopped. Señora Margarita still sat in her slatted chair on the patio. She watched me as I climbed from the car.

"No me recognize, Señora Margarita?"

"No, señor—pero sí, sí—un momento, I do know. You are the patrón, Señor Carlos, No es verdad? I do not see good."

"Sí, Señora, I am he. I'm happy to see you sitting in patio looking so good. But Juan, how is he? Trinidad told me that he is very sick, sick unto death, and I came to see him."

"Don Carlos, many thanks, but now he is better. It went, the fever, and the doctor said he is getting better."

Doña Margarita was grandmother and great-grandmother to part of the de León tribe. The patio in the shade of the palm-leaf roof was her throne room. Here they all passed sooner or later, paid their respects, curtsied and kissed the back of her wrinkled hand. She, in turn, always had a dulce (sweet) for the little ones.

"Where are the boys and the rest?" I asked her.

"Well, Aida is keeping the store this morning. Rafael, Hector, and Andrés are hoeing in the lower field. Tor, the lazy one, went to town. Luis and Miguel are cutting the corn for fodder, and Trinidad is around somewhere."

"Then, con tu permiso, Señora, I'll go find Rafael and Hector—but I did come to see Juan. Is it permitted?"

"Sí, Carlos, but only un momento—no more."

Margarita's white stucco house and store combination stood

exposed on a point of the old river bank. It could be seen for a long way. The lot it stood on, about five hundred feet wide, years before had been along a curved bank of the Rio Grande. The other dimension went to the center of the river. But a flood in a later year had cut a new channel, a short mile to the north, drying up the convex river bend the white home stood on.

Instead of the two or three acres Margarita had had, she now owned nearly fifty acres of undulating, rich made-soil. It was a long, unhandy strip—but it was new land. The family was happy. The boys took hold with gusto, planting it to beans, corn, tomatoes, cantaloupes, and watermelons. They had wanted me to see their melon fields before the summer sun burned them, so I went to see Juan and look over their crops at the same time.

I walked the winding road down the old river bank to the level of the new land and followed the trail down the side of the strip. I found Hector and Rafael at the far end, close to the new river bank—a long walk for me. They greeted me with warmth.

"How can you farm such uneven ground, Rafael?" I asked.

"Well, we do not have tractors, like you. We plowed it with oxen and harrowed it many times with a viga [heavy plank]. Do you see how far the land extends now, Carlos?"

"Yes, I saw it as I walked."

"The river gave it to us—forty acres more."

"And it robbed it from the American side, no? You get to keep this forty acres?"

"Surely, yes. Our deed says 'to the center of the river.' "

"Don't you have to pay anything for this land?"

"No, it's ours. No one else's. It is not government land."

"It is very rich land, too," I said, kicking the ground. "See that tall corn and the big green ears."

"Yes, we are going to cut much corn fodder for the animals.

We're going to have plenty of ears for the tortillas. Come over and see the cantaloupe field."

"Why this string on the stakes?" The field was enclosed with a string tied to each stake about ten inches from the ground.

"That is to keep the coyotes out—that they don't eat the cantaloupes. In the night they come and take bites; from the watermelons, too."

The five-acre block of watermelons also was fenced with a string.

"This does not let the coyotes in?" I asked doubtfully.

"Yes, they won't cross the string."

"Why?"

"I don't know, Carlos, but they won't cross. I think because of the odor of man. They're very suspicious."

"Where did you get all the string? It resembles dried bark."

"It is bark of the jara."

Each strip of bark was about three-eighths of an inch wide and four feet long. The pieces were tied end to end—enough to enclose two five-acre patches of melons—and tied to the stakes. The labor involved had been prodigious. But there were no gouged melons, and they were all covered with handfuls of weeds to keep the hot midday sun from scorching the tender rinds.

When I climbed the road back to the yard, I discovered what was bothering me about the landscape. Russian thistles had taken over everywhere. All the way from western Kansas they had come, as tumbleweeds with the wind. I first saw them on my farm ninety-five years after they were imported from Russia for stock feed. Now they had crossed the Rio Grande and covered northern Mexico with their heavy, dark greenery.

Clementina

SABINO MORALES, ONE OF THREE BROTH-
ers working for me, came to me one afternoon with a question.

"Carlos, wishes Lidia a woman to work for her?"

"Sí, Sabino, I think she should have help. In a little time, comes a new baby. Why?"

"We have a sister in Mexico who is not married, and we too need a woman in our house to work. Clementina said that if la madama wants someone to help her for money, she'd have great pleasure to come. She will stay with us and cook for us."

"I'll tell Lidia about her."

Clementina didn't wait to be asked. She came over, wet, probably by boat somewhere along the river. She came at once to our house to let my wife inspect her.

Lee saw a plain, lean-jawed young woman of twenty-three or twenty-four. She had sun-coarsened features and capable hands; she was neat and unsmiling. She talked slowly, through her nose, in a carrying, strident voice.

Lee and Clementina made a deal that afternoon for part-time work that lasted many years. Clementina was highly satisfactory. She had a good head and was well informed; you had to be careful what you said around her, because she'd check your logic on almost any subject. She didn't encourage humor.

Religiously, Clementina was mixed up, but firm. She had a Mexican blend of Catholicism and superstition. She took her superstitions seriously and defended them with vigor, allowing no mirth on their account. She was perfectly sure that if she failed to do certain things, or did do others, she would be punished. She claimed the house they lived in by the canal was haunted, that she sometimes heard a baby crying in the night.

In her personal plans, she thought a long way ahead. She planned for all of her brothers; their finances, clothes, anything connected with their welfare were her business.

And when Raul, a big, strong youth of eighteen, showed up for work, she decided he'd make a good husband. She took him under her wing along with her brothers out in the tenant house, besieged him with her practical attentions, and finally married him. Seven or eight years between them seemed all right to Raul. He was thoroughly dependable (a trait that Clementina had no doubt observed), and he became my chief tractor driver.

Clementina managed for him, for her three brothers, and for my wife, and then her own baby came. He was an American baby. She had already managed to get Raul and herself naturalized—without my help. (They never became migrants.)

Months passed. The boy's thick, black hair was getting long, and she wouldn't cut it. His scalp was scaly, his hair full of nits; he was miserable.

"Clementina, why no cut you that boy's hair?" I asked. "Are you trying to make a girl out of him?"

"I think he's muy hermoso, very handsome, no?" She laughed through her nose.

"No, I don't."

"Well, Carlos, I don't care if you don't." She laughed noisily again. "But Raul thinks it's all right."

"Very well, maybe. It is not a thing of mine, but, Clementina, you are a good persuader—very persistent, and Raul is very much a boy yet."

It rocked along like that for some weeks. I'd twit her about her "girl." She'd come back with, "No es cosa tuya, it's none of your business." But the weather was getting hotter. The boy was suffering more. He cried a lot. I thought Clementina must be going loco, not to see it.

"Raul," I finally urged, "why don't you take that kid out and cut his hair? I'll lend you the scissors."

Raul laughed. "Clementina will not permit me to cut it."

I stuck my neck out one more time. "Clementina, why in the name of all that's holy don't you cut his hair? You'll kill him." She looked at me disgustedly, as if I should have known better,

"Carlos, to the Virgin de Guadalupe, I promised that if she would let him live, I would not for a year cut his hair. The year is now soon completed and my baby is still alive, no? Isn't that strong, that promise?"

"Yeah, I guess so." I subsided. Let the kid die, then, if she was so stubborn. I'd helped bury babies before.

About three weeks later, Raul asked me for a loan, more money than his wages came to. Clementina and the boy disappeared. In another week she was home again, with her little boy in spanking new clothes and his scaly head shorn.

"Clementina, little José is a fine-looking cristiano, now that you have made a macho, a male, of him."

"Yes," she smiled crookedly. "I took him to the shrine of the Virgin de Guadalupe and prayed. Then I cut his hair."

Cool Water

OUT ON THE RANCHES OF THIS RIO Grande country are many old wells, large square wells dug by men who wanted water badly. Some were dug through fathoms of caliche and needed no shoring. Others were dug partly through earth and walled with square-hewn mesquite logs. Later, heavy timbers were placed across the wide holes in the ground and windmills mounted on them. Still later, wells were drilled where they were wanted with machinery, then encased in iron pipe.

But the well that has my most awed regard is one on the Morales ranch some twenty-five kilometers south and west of Reynosa, Tamaulipas—a well dug by hand through mostly solid caliche for ninety-six feet by the Morales family.

The brothers had been inviting me for some time to visit their home and see their well, of which they were very proud. Finally I drove down taking Kelly and Rikki with me.

I looked over the wooden curbing, down the well's winding length to the small circle of light reflected by water at the bottom. After a moment I turned to the men.

"Sabino, what did you dig this with?" I asked.

"Miguel dug it with the short-handled pick. He is the smallest of us—not so wide."

"Tell me, did you know you would find water here?"

"No."

"Then why did you dig so deep?"

"We had no water," Miguel explained. "We had been borrowing and buying from our neighbor Esquivel."

"But," Enrique interrupted, "Esquivel said he could give no more. The last time we carried from there water, only two gallons, it was the last we could have."

"We were very sad," Sabino went on. "It was bad enough before—five kilómetros to the Esquiveles' hacienda."

"Papá went out and sat himself on the patio. He said nothing," said Enrique.

"Mamá herself laid down on the bed in the corner and cried," said José.

"Oh, we were muy triste, very sorrowful," Luis said, "but Clementina said 'Tomorrow, and God so wishes, we will find some water in that hole before night.' 'But how will we live until tomorrow night?' we asked her."

From the patio Clementina had been listening. She joined us at the well.

"I told these big lazy ones, 'Tomorrow you'll see. Mañana there will be water before sunfall!' "

"When the sunrise came," Miguel continued, "I went to look down in the hole, and something shone back at me like a big eye. 'Water! Water!' I yelled. 'There's water in the hole!' "

"They came running out, all the kids," interrupted their silent, green-eyed daddy, Jesús, "acting foolish—gritando."

"What did you, Jesús?" I asked. "Did you come running too?"

"No, I am too old to get excited. It is as God wishes."

Miguel continued, "When I was lowered to the bottom, I found a little water, maybe two litros. The caliche around the hole was wet, seeping water. With the small can I dipped the water into the big one and signaled those outside to hoist it up."

"What bad water it was!" exclaimed Sabino. "Very ugly, like quinine—mostly caliche. But we drank it, a little for each. It was very muddy and foul."

"I went down to work with my pick, and the brothers raised the dirt and caliche up in the big bucket to the top," said Miguel. "We worked hard that day. We sweated much and drank mud."

"We knew well," added Luis, "that in the next days we would have the trots. That water was very wild—mucho sal de guerra!" They all laughed. "We trotted for some days, but still it was water. Even if it was half Epsom salts. We had no choice."

"Before the night came," Miguel continued, "I was working below in water to the knees. All the time more was seeping in. I wished that I could empty la laguna down there, keep the lake dry, while I was working. Then I could have dug deeper, and we would have more capacidad, more water seeping in." He shrugged and fell silent.

I looked down again into the winding, crooked hole. Like a rope it hung; ninety-six feet. What faith they had had! Tons and tons of rock had come out of the hole.

But now they were raising the water in a ten-gallon can with an automatic valve in its bottom. Attached to the can was a 120-foot rope that ran over a pulley at the top. They kept a pony always saddled with a sawbuck saddle to pull the rope. He had worn a deep path in the sandy earth alongside the corral fence, going back and forth. They now had enough water for themselves and a herd of goats.

"Wish you a trago of water, Don Carlos?"

"Yes, I very much do."

They sent the can down to the "lake" at the bottom. My drink was satisfying; sweet and cool.

CHAPTER TWO

The
Cultures

MEXICAN TRIBAL CULTURES ALL RESTED on one grain—corn—while our culture was built on a great variety.

One grain (corn); one climate (warm); one language (Spanish); one religion (Catholic); one social pattern (paternal) produced the Mexican as we know him.

The Spanish conquest of Mexico was primarily to furnish gold for Spain, second to convert the natives to Christianity. Spanish officials remained and carved out their fiefs, and their followers consorted with the native women, learned to like tortillas, and took up their cultures.

North Americans came from everywhere, bringing their women and children. Their primary purpose was to establish homes, their secondary one to be free to think. They were from many climates, many regions, many languages, and many social ideas. Nothing was dominant. They pushed the native inhabitants to one side.

This statement is too brief to develop the effects of these characteristics on the two peoples. It is enough to say that the two peoples have existed with only the wild river between them, and contacts have often been somewhat abrasive.

The gap between the twentieth-century technology of this country and the primitive innocence of an untaught Mexican from the country was sometimes almost too great to grasp. When the wetback crossed the Rio Grande, in one step he set himself down among strange people, speaking a strange language, in a country filled with roads and radios, trucks and tractors, can openers and cars. He brought with him his own culture, language, and religion; deep-rooted superstitions and fears; an avid, childlike curiosity, and at times an almost total ignorance of our modern technology.

Susto

"WHAT'S THE MATTER?" LEE ASKED WHEN I came in to breakfast.

"What the devil does 'susto' really mean?" I replied.

"Who's scared now?"

"It's that doggoned Juan. He got susto-ed last night over at the tenant house, and he's got the whole bunch susto-ed this morning."

"Is that why you've all been standing around out there?"

"Yes. I've heard that word all my life. It seems the more ignorant a Mexican is, the more he uses it—the more he gets susto-ed. You never hear an educated Mexican use it. Sometimes they say 'sustado,' sometimes 'asustado.' I wonder if there's a difference."

"What did Juan see?" Lee asked.

"He says he saw Miguel go past his bunk and outside the house, and the door didn't open. When Miguel didn't come back in, Juan finally got up to check Miguel's bunk, and Miguel was in it, asleep. Then Juan got susto-ed. He told the rest of them, and they all heard noises the rest of the night. The nitwit says he's not going to sleep over there another night."

Lee had found the little Spanish-English dictionary. "It says that 'susto' means 'fright,' and 'asustar' means 'to frighten.'"

The kids had come down to breakfast and were listening.

"They're always talking about a baby crying," Kelly said.

"Clementina talks about babies while she's here ironing," added Sister. "She says there are two, one out in the field west of the house. She bugs out her eyes and whispers."

"We haven't heard anything about that for two years," Lee objected.

"I have," said little Dixie, "lots, from Clementina."

"I hoped when I put those bunks in there, that would be the last of it," I grumbled.

"Well," suggested Lee, "maybe there's something to it."

"Naw, there isn't," I said. "Those noises are nothing but sparking possums under the low floor."

"That's enough to scare anyone," she commented.

"But these are grown men, not kids. They say the house is asustado. The dictionary says 'frightened.' The house is frightened?"

"Well, Carrol. You know very well that means 'haunted.'"

"Then the only way to get rid of this ghost is to burn down the house?"

"Yes," Lee agreed, "A story like that goes on forever."

When Clementina and Raul lived there—before I put in the bunks—she was very positive about the ghost and queer noises. She never stayed alone; Raul was always there with her. Raul too said he saw a ghostly thing parading around outside once, although he never threatened to leave. But then, he was my tractor driver, and had more sense than some.

I passed the house many times at night, going over to shut off the irrigating water; I never saw anything. Old Leonel, a practical Mexican American with no poetry in him, lived there alone for five years once.

But no Mexican national will sleep there alone.

The Withered Tree

ONE DAY WHEN BILL, A NEIGHBOR, WAS disking he found an orange tree out in the center of his orchard that was covered with white goatshair vines. It was in very bad shape. The rest of the trees were healthy and green. Why Bill or his father hadn't noticed it sooner, he didn't know. At noon he spoke to his regular man.

"Amadeo, there's an orange tree in the grove that looks like it is going to die. It hasn't been cleared around for several years."

"Yes, patrón, there is one such."

"Why have you never hoed around it? The vines are killing it."

"I know, but the mojados you had before me never cleaned it. They told me not to; that one is asustado."

"Why should it be asustado?"

"Under there is buried a man."

"Such a story I never heard!"

"Come, I'll show to you the grave."

They walked from the road out to the white, woolly tree, through the deep tilth.

"See that mound, patrón? There is buried a man. Your men who worked here before me said that your neighbor—an American, white, very bad—killed his wetback and buried him there."

Then Bill remembered that years before—more years than the neglect of the tree showed—a wetback working for old man Stolberg had disappeared. The old man had owed him some money and wanted to pay him, but had not been able to find him since he hadn't known his name or where in Mexico he came from. No one ever spoke of it anymore.

The workers must have been talking about it all this time, enlarging the story and handing it on to newcomers among them. Now they had him buried under the tree's spreading branches.

How could old man Stolberg have carried a corpse from his place, a mile down the road, and out into the center of Bill's orchard to bury it—without being seen, to boot? But if there was a body there, Bill wanted the authorities to know about it at once. He called the sheriff's office. Two deputies came out with shovels. One crossed himself before disturbing the place.

After trimming away limbs and vines, they began to dig. The soil did seem to be looser, more friable under the low "mound." Citrus and vine roots ran through it in a tangle, but the soil looked as if it might have been moved at some time. They dug to a reasonable depth for a body, but found no bones. As the deputies left, the one who had crossed himself genuflected anyway.

Bill's man made the sign of the cross and refused to clean around the tree. No other wetback who came on the place would do it, either. They all crossed themselves and detoured around it. Bill finally cleared it out himself.

"Friends, Romans, and Countrymen"

THE MEN HAD ASKED ME FOR MANY years if I could give them more work to do when cotton picking was done. I thought about it, and finally one time asked, "If I plant broomcorn, will you come over and harvest it?" "Seguro que sí" was the answer, so I did.

When picking cotton, they had looked for a private place to

empty their bowels. The cotton plants were too low to provide privacy. But broomcorn is tall, and you can't see far in it. Privacy is where you are. My sons Kelly and Rikki had made the mistake a few times of not looking where they were stepping, and had run afoul. Kelly was always easy-going, but Rikki was just naturally imperious. People had to crap—his word—where he wanted them to. "Go yourself to the end of the field somewhere," he would shout. "Don't leave it in the broomcorn!" The men would smile, but Kelly and Rikki still found the piles in any handy place.

Working along a broomcorn row one morning, Rikki stepped in another pile. He was furious. He called the men over to the field lateral, where he could stand a little higher than they. The near-failing grades he always got in Spanish in school had never deterred him. Within the year, he had been studying Shakespeare's plays. Now he took his tone from Mark Antony's funeral speech.

"Amigos—mejicanos—mojados! Mi prestas a mí tus orejas. Los males que vivi—ah—después—ah—"

Friends—Mexicans—wetbacks! Lend me your ears. The evil men do, lives after them—

"Ah, qué Rikki!" The men giggled.

"Don't scatter your crap in the broomcorn field! Carry yourself to the ditch!" he pointed dramatically. The men laughed harder.

I won't try to reproduce the conglomerate he used after that. It was accompanied by punching motions at the heavens with his fists, showing his teeth, and other queer gestures and sounds. He yelled and pointed. He knew a few foul Spanish words and used them freely and sonorously. He got red in the face.

"Go over there, dammit, to do your crapping! Not *here* where we have to walk—over *there!*" They were now attentive and impressed. They looked toward the ditch obediently, following his pointing arm with each thrust.

"Don't—leave—your—crap—in—the—broomcorn!" They all stared gravely and nodded.

Then they went and did as they pleased.

The boys managed to avoid any further accidents. Their talents were sharpening. But one day Rikki came upon an area in the center of the field where a giant nest of big red ants had killed all surrounding vegetation. The mound was bare and smooth. The ants were taking a siesta, all in the hole. It was an ideal place, and someone had used it in the very near past to lay an egg.

Rikki surveyed it with disgust. Then he saw possibilities. The artist in him took over. The coloring and background were just right. The materials—his sharp broomcorn knife and sunflowers in bloom—were at hand.

He cut a quantity of flowers, cropping the stems close so the flowers would lie flat, face up. These he placed carefully in an intricate pattern around the pile, using sizes and shades effectively. He outlined a casket-like rectangle with the beautiful yellow and brown flowers. He trimmed a long sunflower stalk and a short one and tied them firmly together in the form of a cross, and this he planted at the head of the "casket."

Rikki surveyed his handiwork with satisfaction. A dead man with a proper burial! It was still siesta time in the nest, so the ants hadn't disturbed his work. He left his masterpiece and returned to cutting off broomcorn heads.

An hour or so later there came, through the still air of the broomcorn field, a wild shriek, then sustained screams of terror. It was a man's voice, nerve-shattering.

"Ai-yai—ai-yai—!"The men rushed toward it from over the field. It went on and on, and Kelly and Rikki ran to join the others.

Rafael stood, legs spraddled in a terror-stricken crouch, his eyes riveted on Rikki's "grave"—hat askew, tearing at his forelock with one hand, the other fist raised in the air and keeping cadence with his scream. He was surrounded by silent, watching men. His falsetto rose and fell.

"Ai-yai—ai-yai—ai-yai—!"

The ants had finished their siesta. They were crawling all over the mound, making the flowers wiggle.

Rikki began to feel guilty. He tried to keep the men calm and to still Rafael.

"Rafael, can't you see, Rafael, the man is dead. Look, there's no danger," and he poked the "corpse" with a stalk of broom-corn.

"Ai-yai—ai-yai—" Rafael didn't see Rikki. Rafael didn't even know he himself was yelling. Rikki jerked down his waving arm and shook him.

"Rafael! Callete la boca! 'tá muerto! Muy pestoso!" His Spanish failed him. "Shut up, you damned fool!" he roared. "Can't you see? He's dead! He stinks! He's dead!"

Rafael's stark terror gradually lessened into shuddering sobs. He stumbled to the pickup and sat on the running board with a vacant look. The men slipped back quietly to their work.

Kelly and Rikki looked at each other. They were unnerved themselves. They left the scene silently.

"Maybe it wasn't such a good idea," Rikki ventured after a while.

Curiosity

DO YOU THINK A WINDOW IS MADE TO look out through, to let in air and light? Our curious wetbacks believed that a window is made to look *in* through. One window in Lee's and my bedroom faced south, overlooking the patio and the swimming pool beyond. It was handy; Lee or I could lie on the bed and watch the kids swimming.

The wetbacks would troop across the patio at will, day or night, taking a short cut from the west road to the barn. We could hear their feet on the tiling.

They never failed to glance in the window as they went by, or hesitate and take a longer look. They would come to the window and talk to me while I was in bed recuperating from an illness. Or they'd stop to watch the kids in the pool, laugh at their antics, glance in the window at us to share the joke. Sometimes Lee was caught unprepared; she'd be furious.

A package or a sack from town was irresistible. Its contents had to be discovered and examined. What could it be, so important that it had to be wrapped?

Our R.F.D. mailbox was at the side of the road north of the house, on a short post, mounted low so that our small children could bring in the mail. We were all taught that a mailbox is private, between the U.S. government and the subscriber, inviolate government property protected by federal law. You just didn't monkey with someone else's mailbox.

But there was nothing like this in Mexico. That mailbox has a door on it. A door is meant to be opened—No? That's why it was made—No? If there is no lock on it, it's all right to open it—No?

Every morning a long string of hands coming to work passed by the mailbox. The first one would open it, stoop, and look in. Empty! He'd slam it shut. The next would open it, stoop, and look in to see why the first one had. Empty! Slam. The third would follow suit, and the fourth, and the fifth . . . We heard this metallic cacophony every morning, every evening.

But how were we to teach them not to touch, without hurting their feelings?

Wetback Banking

I WAS STANDING IN THE SHADED PATIO of Doña Margarita's store at Quatro Palmas, talking to some of her sons and a neighbor who also picked cotton for me. We were looking out over the lowlands where the river once had flowed. Another neighbor, again one of my wetbacks, came into sight walking across his adjoining land toward the river. He had a shovel across his shoulder. His destination seemed to be a clump of huisaches.

Nicolás laughed, snorting through his juicy nose. The others looked at him questioningly.

"Who knows?" he said. "Maybe old Alfonso has his money buried there and is going to look at it." They all snickered. I didn't get it.

"Does Alfonso bury his money?" I asked.

"Yes," they told me, "but not in the daylight."

I mulled this over. "Qué curioso! Why doesn't he take it to a bank?" I knew that he earned quite a bit when he picked for me.

"To the bank?" They looked scornful. "There is only one in town. They just rob a poor cristiano there. Only un sonso would carry his money to the bank. Son bandidos!"

"What do you boys and Grandmamá do with your money?" I pursued. They laughed as if I too were sonso.

"Everybody does this!"

"What if you forget where you dug the hole?"

"Yes, like that it sometimes happens, or an evil one watches where a poor one buries his money, hits him in the head, and throws him in the river. But it is best to bury it on your own land. You know where it is then."

With this wisdom slightly digested, I asked, "Do you boys do that with all the money I give you for picking my cotton?"

"Seguro que sí, Don Carlos. Of course. There is no other way."

ONE MORNING WHEN I WAS IN EDINBURG I ran into Ralph, one of our bankers. We went for coffee.

"Carrol, do you know a Mexican by the name of Fidencio?" he asked, after we found a place at the counter together. "I think he lives out near you."

"Yes, I've known Fidencio for thirty years or more. He hollers when he talks."

"That's the fellow. Nice old man."

"Yes, he's a fine old fellow; but he can't even write his own name."

"I didn't know that. He's always well dressed and clean."

"That's his wife's doing," I said. "She's kind of aristocratic; careful about the way she walks and talks. A lady. She may be able to write."

"That's her. I want to tell you about her," he said. "She came into the bank over a year ago with several hundred dollars in bills. In a paper sack! She wanted to leave the sack in the bank so no one could steal it. We counted the money and opened an account for her—and kept the sack. She was uneasy about that.

"I hadn't seen her since, until day before yesterday. She came in as soon as Charley opened the doors. In fact, she'd been standing outside waiting for the doors to open."

"That sounds like Sari, all right," I told him. "Always on the ball and pushing. She's serious. She doesn't see a joke; leaves all that nonsense to Fidencio."

"She walked right up to my window," Ralph continued, "and looked me in the eye sort of accusingly. 'Do you me know? Remember me?'

" 'I sure do,' I said, 'You're Mrs. Casteñada.'

"Some of the fire left her eye. But she came right back at me before I got settled. 'Is that money I gave to you still here? Where is it?'

" 'Yes, I think so.' I smiled, but she didn't see anything funny. So as not to arouse her any more, I added, 'I'm sure it is. I'll go see.'

"I went to the books, checked, and came back to the window. She hadn't moved. 'It's still here. You haven't taken any out or put any more in,' I pointed out.

" 'No, I know,' she answered, 'that is correct. It is still here— all of it?'

"I nodded. 'Why, yes, Mrs. Casteñada.' Then, as she kept looking at me, I asked, 'Do you want it? I'll give it to you.'

" 'No.' She relaxed more and half-smiled as if I were a child. 'No, señor, if it's still here, I don't want it.'

"She walked straight out of the bank as if she'd caught me in something dirty. Carrol, I felt guilty; I still do, kinda!"

"Well, Ralph," I laughed, "old Sari is like that. She's a fine woman, saving and economical. She's saved old Fidencio money. They've got a nice little home out there; painted green."

It was ten years before I heard the rest of the story.

It seems someone had left about nine hundred dollars to the old couple. They talked about what to do with all that money.

Sari wanted to put it in a bank. She tried to keep herself up to date, modern in her outlook. But Fidencio wanted to bury it. It was safe in the ground, he held, with a peon's reasoning. He'd lived in Mexico during those interminable revolutions; maybe he'd taken part. Anyway, he had seen plenty of banditry. In the ground it was safe; he knew.

To resolve the difference of opinion, they divided the bills equally. Sari took her half hesitantly to the bank. Wasn't that what banks were for? Police all around?

Old Fidencio put his half in a glass jar, took a shovel that night, and buried it out under the ebony tree.

A year passed, and Fidencio got to worrying about his money. Maybe it was gone; maybe someone had seen him bury it! So he dug it up, brought the jar to the house, and opened it. The money was still there, all right, but it had rotted. It fell apart in his hands. Qué lástima!

Sari saw it. It was the next morning that she rushed over to the bank to see if her part of the money was still there.

A *Practical Joker*

I NEVER SAW A MEXICAN NATIONAL inflict a practical joke on anyone. I've heard of a few, very few. I don't know, of course, but I suspect the reason is a low boiling point, an ever present consciousness of needing to keep one's best foot forward. A broad joke at his own expense is not likely to be taken lightly by a Mexican.

Sam Wilson, a neighbor, had two wetbacks who were practical jokers working for him one summer. They played it safe, though, and played jokes only on each other. One I've always remembered, for it was enough to make any ordinary Mexican think of taking revenge at once.

Margarito was the victim. Victor thought it up and carried it through. Victor was Sam's best worker, used regularly for tractor work where the driver needed good judgment. Margarito was all right for the tractor job that day, though—cutting cotton stalks.

It had been a wet spring and summer. The yield had been very light, but the stalks had grown seven and eight feet tall, their stems the thickness of a hoe handle. The foliage was dense; a man walking through the field was invisible to another walking only two rows from him.

Margarito was using a rolling stalk-cutter, four blades welded to a steel drum of equal length, long enough to cut two rows at a time. A crude affair, the stalk-cutter was efficient on the thick stalks. The cutting edges of the blades being equidistant from each other, each blade met the ground with a tooth-rattling jolt. It was a rough, jerky job, but little technical knowledge was needed to keep the tractor on a pair of rows and to be careful not to fall off the seat. To fall off would mean the certainty of being chewed up by the blades.

Margarito, not traveling very fast, was feeling good on the cool September afternoon. A good singer who knew lots of songs, he was enjoying himself thoroughly and letting the world know that he was happy as he rocked along the quarter-mile rows. The sound of his singing carried above the noise of the cutter.

Victor was at the bunkhouse. He was thinking. He had already rejected several projects for having some fun with Margarito. At last his eyes began to twinkle and he began to search for materials.

He found a piece of three-inch angle iron six feet long, a three-foot piece of two-by-four, and an armload of discarded clothes from the bunkhouse floor. He wired the two-by-four to the angle iron, forming a cross. He tied an old pair of khaki pants to it, and a blue jacket with the cross bar through the sleeves. He wired an old leather boot to the foot of the cross, and a straw hat to the top. He stuffed it all with dried johnson grass. At a distance it might look like a scarecrow—or a man, if one were in a hurry.

Victor carried his scarecrow out to the center of the field, four rows ahead of where Margarito was cutting. He waited until Margarito was near the other end of the field, then laid the straw man lengthwise in a row on which Victor would be coming back. The foliage of the tall cotton was dense enough so that Margarito would not see the dummy from the tractor seat, and the wheels of the tractor would not find it, for they traveled between the rows. Victor backed off until he was out of sight, and listened.

The cutter hit the straw man with a crashing and clanking—much louder than Victor had expected. The singing stopped. The tractor came roaring toward him. Panicking, he started running across the rows, tripped on the horizontal limbs of the cotton stalks, and fell flat. The tractor, with its wide cutter jolting behind, seemed to be following him.

Margarito was having troubles, too. Something terrible had happened. The clanking behind, the erratic jerking of the tractor by its own draw bar, the bouncing of the springy seat, all unnerved him. He threw a frantic glance over his shoulder. Madre de Díos! Hat, shoe, and clothing of a man! The jacket was caught on a cutter blade, rolling over with it each time.

Margarito's first thought was to flee. He'd killed a man. His second thought was to flee, too, but a tractor in high working gear is a hard thing to flee.

The steering wheel jerked sideways across the rows. The tractor was describing a wide circle through the tall stalks. Margarito turned the wheel. The tractor went the other way and made a giant S in the field. It was nearing the vicinity of the dead man again. Chingao! He didn't want to run over him again!

Margarito was beginning to get hold of his nerves, though. It occurred to him to change gears. The tractor slowed down, and he got it to go down a pair of rows again. This made for the familiar rhythmic motion. He could think still better. He decided that it wasn't wise to leave the tractor. After all, it wasn't his fault; the man himself was somehow to blame, too.

He could see where he had been circling, so he decided to return to the scene of the accident. Chingao! The man must be dead. Perhaps he had been dead before Margarito had hit him! Ojalá que sí! He slowed the tractor more and eased up to the corpse.

Some scattered metal and wood; a smashed straw hat, a boot, torn pants. No man. Margarito studied the objects. He glanced around. His peripheral vision caught movement at the far end of the field. A man walked there. It looked like Victor.

This demanded more thought. Margarito was calm now. He lined out on the rows he had been cutting when the accident had happened and continued his work.

Soon he felt much better. He decided to mention the incident to nobody; never to Victor. Before long a song, clear and high, was wafted aloft on the breeze.

Wild People

FRANK WAS NOT A FARMER. HE HAD A regular job, but he owned some land that was lying idle, so he had it planted to cotton. The cotton was open.

A neighbor's field alongside his was being picked by an unusually strange group of people from south of Mexico City somewhere. There were about eleven or twelve of them. They didn't talk much, and no one could understand their dialect when they did. They were squat and twisted, all under five feet, with deep-set eyes and overhanging eyebrows. They were terribly shy, a wild shyness. You couldn't get close to them; they'd run away, then stand and watch you.

Frank asked his neighbor to start them on Frank's patch when they got through picking the adjoining field. When he came home from work, he went over to see how they were progressing. While he was there, a small child fell from the top of the cotton trailer to the ground. He cut his head on a piece of gravel; it bled profusely. His people didn't do anything for the cut, but chattered quietly at him for falling. He didn't cry.

Frank caught him and tried to wipe away the blood with a handkerchief, but the boy fought like an animal. The others stood at a distance and watched, like a bunch of cattle when you doctor a calf for screw worms.

Later Frank brought them a large watermelon. They backed away, afraid or distrusting. He left. At a distance, he looked back. They had surrounded the melon, were tearing it apart with their hands and eating it.

Frank decided they were hungry. He told his young wife, Sharon, to cook up a pot of beans. He carried the pot out to them himself. Again he couldn't get near them. They just scampered and watched him. He set the pot down. When he looked back, they were wolfing the beans just as they had the melon.

The next day he and Sharon gathered up all the old shoes and clothes they could find around the house. He took them out to the pickers, who backed away. He left the things in a pile by the cotton trailer. From a distance he could see that they had torn the pile apart and were waving various articles around with a soft buzz of conversation. The next time he went out the clothes were being worn; some shoes were mismatched, but the people didn't care.

The day after, a small boy, ten or twelve, walked in the open kitchen door. Sharon was alone. The boy held a flat can of sardines in front of him with both hands. He advanced about halfway to Sharon and stood waiting.

Sharon didn't know what was going on. She spoke to him but he didn't make a sound, just looked at her steadily. He looked as if he might turn and fly if she made a move.

"Is it some kind of offering?" she wondered. "A gift in return for the clothes? Or does he want to trade it for something?"

She moved toward him. He held his ground, still holding the can forward with both hands, watching her warily. She reached slowly for the can. He made no move to avoid her. She took it; he relinquished it, but continued to stand with his empty hands outstretched as if still holding it. Sharon stood holding the can, wondering what to do. At last she had an idea.

She found her can opener and began to open the can. The boy watched her carefully, his hands still extended. She took the lid halfway off and held out the can to him. He didn't reach for it, so she placed it in his open hands.

He turned and walked silently out the door. She watched him walk steadily through the gate, still holding the tin with both hands.

The Queréteños

THE QUERÉTEÑOS APPEARED AND HUNG around the community for several days looking for work. They had evidently been across the river before, and they wanted certain conditions met before they'd go to work: to be taken to church early on Sundays and brought back later so they could pick cotton on Sunday afternoons; to be paid on Saturdays; to work only five and a half days a week. The requests were not unreasonable, but cotton wasn't yet open much, and most owners didn't want to be bothered with them. Flemming needed pickers, though, so finally he took them on.

They were small, averaging under five feet and about 110 pounds, with round heads and faces and little feet in dainty huaraches. Their four-cornered hats of woven palm leaves came to a peak in the center, and were cleaner than the heavy sweat-stained hats of the ordinary wetbacks. Their clothes were washed-out white but not ragged.

The Queréteños were as quick as monkeys, active and inquisitive. They liked to catch snakes and put them through acrobatic routines. When they got through playing with a rattler they snapped his head off like you'd crack a blacksnake whip. They would go into rattlesnake-infested cotton fields that other Mexicans were afraid to pick.

They were at home in the water. When pushed by la chota, they simply jumped into a barrow pit, drainage ditch, or canal, disappeared into the rushes or cattails, no matter how foul the water was with algae, and stayed out of sight for hours.

People were always surprised to meet Mexicans who couldn't speak Spanish. The Queréteños were proud; they weren't interested in learning other languages—let others learn theirs. Only one of them, Luis, could speak a little broken Spanish. He kept their official picking weights and did their business.

They were very polite. When talking to any outsider, they held their hats in both hands to one side and bowed from the hips. This was a bit embarrassing to any stranger, but especially so to Efrén, a young fellow who worked for Flemming and did the weighing for the little Indians when they picked for el patrón. They called Efrén "Señor Amo"—"Mr. Boss"—and never failed to bow to him in all the weeks they were there. The Queréteños didn't relax much with strangers—although they played and wrestled and cackled joyously together—but they liked Efrén. The glittering black eyes in their recessed sockets registered a happy understanding with him from the first.

Flemming spoke no Spanish, the Queréteños no English, so the burden of communicating fell to Efrén and to little Luis with his pidgin Spanish. It made for a lot of chattering.

One day they were all making an unusual amount of noise. The figures didn't agree for the picking one of the little Indians had done. Flemming picked this delicate moment to breeze in. He listened for a while, came to a decision, and entered the fray.

"Let me in on this," he said, brushing his way to the center. He forgot momentarily that he could speak only English, and that, worse yet, the little Indian making all the fuss could speak only his Queréteño dialect. El patrón had little understanding of the issue, and only Efrén could understand his blusterings. It took Flemming some little time to realize this truth. But he did, so he switched his efforts from the Indian to Efrén.

He demanded Efrén's attention. He told Efrén how the bull ate the cabbage.

Efrén told Luis, in characteristically polite Spanish, how the bull ate the cabbage.

Luis then told the lesser Indian, in apparently understandable noises, how the bull ate the cabbage.

Number Two Indian was little, but he was adamant. He returned the cabbage to his compadre who could speak Spanish. Luis handed the cabbage politely back to Efrén, who in turn laid it down for Flemming.

Flemming chewed the cud for a little and passed it back again to Efrén, who gave it courteously to Luis. Luis chattered it to Indian number two, who masticated it noisily for a while. It worked up pressure and came right back to Luis, who flipped it to Efrén, who shunted it to Flemming.

It went the round a few more times, losing some of its substance. The residue was left with el patrón.

Flemming suddenly saw the absurdity of the situation: Four men using three languages to resolve a small matter, each trying to stay within the bounds of courtesy in his own language, there in the shade of that wide, trashy chinaberry tree.

El patrón smiled. Number Two Indian smiled. Luis and Efrén smiled. El patrón laughed out loud. They all laughed. El patrón's belly shook.

Flemming had a bright idea when the laughter subsided. He suggested that they should all have some fun—continue their four-cornered conversation, only about some ordinary topic. They batted the idea down the line until everybody understood it. Everybody thought it would be fun. But they couldn't understand each other fast enough to agree on what to talk about.

Can It Talk Spanish?

FAUSTINO, A SHORT LITTLE GUY OF ABOUT forty-five, came from the mountains of Durango. He arrived on this side of the river alone one night. He had a straw hat, collarless shirt, white pants, and huaraches made from an old rubber tire. He immediately got a job picking cotton. He was a veteran cotton picker, practically illiterate, and thoroughly rural—mountain rural.

He earned more money in a week's time than he had seen in several years. He came to town Saturday to buy necessities. He'd heard from his compadres of a store where they sold U.S. army surplus cheap.

In the patrón's bunkhouse Faustino had been initiated into the delightful versatility of the radio. He had never seen one before. The exuberant Mexican music coming across the river on the air waves delighted him; he never got enough of it. The men assured him that a radio was easily bought in town, and Faustino determined to own one.

The store was full of wetbacks, the clerks very busy. Faustino was patient, and this gave him plenty of time to examine at a distance the row of radios on the shelf. He was going to buy, but he didn't want to be pushed. A small blue one seemed to be making all the noise. Faustino viewed it from different angles, at length. He didn't want anyone to see his interest, but he was highly obvious.

Ralph Berry, the store's owner, had come home to his wife and two kids as a World War II veteran without a job. He'd been a store clerk before the war, and he and a friend bought a stock of used and new armed forces surpluses, opened a store, and sold at a small profit to the Mexican nationals who had swarmed into the Valley. The partners were energetic. They kept the store open from early morning to midnight seven days a week; they wanted to be ready for any wetback, any time, and wetbacks were afoot and unaccustomed to American time schedules.

Ralph watched Faustino from his place at the cash register and let him look. But after a time Ralph's patience wore out. He flipped the key, left the register, and ambled over.

"Do you wish to buy a radio?" he asked the self-conscious customer.

"Sí, señor," Faustino answered gratefully. "I want a little one, if I have enough money."

"Do you it want—the one you are looking at?"

"Who knows?" Faustino countered. "Will it play music?"

"Seguro que sí." Ralph dialed away from the speaking voice to an American music program. The little radio blared. Faustino's eyes sparkled. Ralph displayed it seductively—softly, then loudly, from station to station. Faustino listened for a while.

"How much do you wish for it?" he asked.

"It's only six pesos—no more," Ralph replied. Faustino listened longer. He was deeply satisfied with the radio, especially with its volume. Then, trying not to show Ralph his eagerness, he asked, "Can it talk Spanish?"

Ralph did a double-take but hid his surprise.

"Seguro que sí. Sure it will."

Faustino was already peeling dollar bills from his roll. "Then I'll buy it."

Cigarette Lighter

CHICO WAS UNUSUALLY SHORT, AN INDIAN from the mountains of Zacatecas. Here in the Valley he worked for a cattleman. Simple, rough work around the feed lots he could do well. He worked steadily with no breathers or coffee breaks. He must have been totally illiterate—a Stone Age character.

The border patrol picked him up at work one day, took him by Ray's house in town to get his pay, and took him to the corral for repatriation. The next morning Chico was back—sitting in Ray's yard swing, as usual, waiting for Ray to get up and out. They started for the cattle pens in Ray's car.

For years Chico had smoked self-built cigarettes of corn-shucks and black tobacco. But the trip to Mexico had been good for him; he felt expansive. For the first time, he blew himself to a package of American cigarettes. Riding up the highway toward the cattle pens, Chico pulled the crumpled package from his pocket and offered Ray a cigarette. Ray didn't smoke, so he waved his finger sideways, the sign for no. He spoke no Spanish, Chico no English.

Chico stuck a cigarette in his own mouth and put the package back in his pocket. Then he just sat there. It bothered Ray that Chico didn't light his cigarette. After a period during which they glanced at each other intermittently, it dawned on Ray that Chico didn't have a match. Ray reached out to the dashboard and pushed in the cigarette lighter. When it popped out again, hot, Ray pulled it from the socket and offered it to Chico. Chico looked at it, took it, examined it. The lighter cooled, unused. Ray stuck it back in the receptacle. He wondered why Chico hadn't lighted his cigarette with it while it was hot.

The lighter popped out again. Ray passed it to Chico again. Chico looked at it. The red spot in its center intrigued him. He stuck his middle finger into the lighter to feel it. It was a close fit.

All hell broke loose. Chico knew what to do with the lighter then—let go! But *it* wouldn't let go; it stuck to his finger. He writhed with pain. He would have jumped out of the car, but the door was shut—and his hands were occupied.

The lighter dropped off finally when he jerked his hand hard. The end of his finger was cooked white.

Part of Chico's cigarette was still in his mouth, but it took another session with the lighter for him to learn to use it. Chico was a very intelligent Mexican, but it's a great jump from Stone Age to modern technology. It's not really funny when you think about it.

Embryonic Chauffeur

I HAD JUST COME OUT OF THE BANK IN Edinburg and stepped off the curb to cross the street, when from my left I heard a clanking crash, ending with a shriek of steel on steel. Between me and the source of the sound, a few cars in diagonal parking places on the north side of Harriman Street blocked my line of sight.

A slender young man shot suddenly into view from between

two cars—a man wearing work clothes and a Mexican straw hat. He ran diagonally southeast across the street to the mouth of a paved alley and disappeared at top speed.

I jumped back up on the curb to see what on earth he was running from. The front end of a green pickup was hanging in midair over the sidewalk. The truck had entered the parking space so fast that it had jumped the curb and had struck the meter post in flight, bent the post over, and come to rest with the front of the pickup in the air. I hurried back to a point where I was in line with the alley, but the man was gone.

By its license number, the police located the truck's owner— Henry Westland, a farmer south and east of town. A few weeks later I met Henry in town.

"How come your man was in town with that truck?" I asked. He seemed to enjoy telling about it. The young wetback had been shown by his compadres how to operate the pickup, and had driven it a little on the field roads on farm errands. It was enough to make him think he was an expert; he liked it. He was out of cigarettes.

"He enjoyed American makes," Henry explained. "I wasn't around, so he took the pickup and went sailing into town. I expect he was coming too fast, saw the parking place, turned in, and forgot how to stop the truck. You know, Carrol," he added, "I haven't seen that wetback since. Neither have any of the other wetbacks."

"I saw him," I told Henry. "He was so terrified by the trouble he was in, once that pavement was under his huaraches he just kept going."

"I'll bet the clatter of those free feet on the asphalt sounded good to him," Henry laughed. "I'd like to see him again—I still owe him that week's wages."

"He'll show up, maybe next year."

"Oh, I'm not worried about that. I'd just like to hear his account of his shopping trip."

"Did he hurt the pickup much?"

"It was scratched up some, but for my uses it's all right."

"Well," I told him, "I saw him run. He accelerated. It didn't take him long at all to hit top speed. But he wasn't so scared that he didn't know which way to run!"

"He was going south fast, was he?"

Death on the Railroads

RIGHT AFTER THE BIG INFLUX OF WET-backs began in the early forties, there was a rash of accidents around the Valley in which wetbacks were killed on the railroad tracks. In every case the trainmen either didn't see the man at all or else saw him lying between the rails when it was too late to stop. In a couple of cases, a Mexican was lying on the track with his head on a rail—as if placed there deliberately for a quick death, or as if he had used the rail for a pillow.

Some people thought they were drunk. Others thought that they had just lain down to sleep, partly drunk or tired. But why on the railroad tracks?

Sometimes the authorities thought they had been victims of violence and had been put there to hide the evidence of a murder or robbery. There were few clues after the body had been hit by a train. No one knew who they were; investigations were not prolonged and soon were forgotten.

Gradually a reason for the phenomenon became generally accepted in the Valley. I presume it was explained by wetbacks who hadn't been killed. Most of the dead men had come from districts in Mexico where there were few, if any, railroads. They had believed, perhaps correctly, that rattlesnakes would not cross the rails to disturb them while they slept.

The deaths seemed to taper off after one night in which two men were killed at different places. The wetbacks became aware of the danger, and the more experienced ones warned newcomers about the real purpose of the steel rails.

The New Car Owner

IT IS HARD TO IMAGINE THE HUNGER OF a man in his prime to sit behind a steering wheel. A man who has watched others, even young boys, drive up and down the roads; a man middle-aged and getting older who has always been denied the feeling of being in control of the power and speed of a vehicle; a man used to riding on a donkey with his wife and kids trailing behind on foot, or to loading the family into a big-wheeled oxcart to go cross-country for a Sunday visit— Simón Lemus was such a man.

Simón had worked for John Grady for several years. After the first year, he had brought his wife and little boy over. His three younger children had been born there. John was thoroughly satisfied with Simón. Neighboring wetbacks might sneak off to tour the northern states on work safaris, but in order to hold Simón John had rented him twenty acres on shares.

Simón's family picked the cotton as it opened. One year when he had accumulated and sold two bales he asked John to let him keep the rent money temporarily, so he could buy himself a pickup truck.

Simón was going to be a man of affairs. He had been patient, but the distances were far and his family was growing. He had looked forward anxiously to the time when he could take the wheel of his own truck. Saturday afternoon he went to town. He had picked out a used blue pickup. The car dealer was waiting for him with the pickup all polished up. Simón paid too much, but he was satisfied. He drove home, gathered up his family and a few other wetbacks, and took them for a ride to show off the new possession.

His wife, Pilar, and the three younger children went to Morelis in Mexico to visit her parents the next week. Three of Simón's buddies came over that Saturday afternoon to inspect the new pickup. They all decided to go over to the highway and up to a little colonia beer joint. The battery was down; the new pickup wouldn't start.

They were disappointed. None of el patrón's family was home, but their son Roy's pickup was in the barnyard. Why not use it? It started and they all piled in—five in the cab's seat.

Two hours later they started gaily for home. They had underestimated the potency of the beer and partying. They hit a loaded truck head on.

John hurried over as soon as he heard. A local man had cut them out of the cab with a torch, and others had laid the five out on the shoulder side by side. Simón was dead. His son Oskar had a broken leg. The other men were badly injured, but would live.

Pilar and the little ones came home Sunday to an unexpectedly empty house. She had a foreboding of disaster. She hurried over to the big house.

John was dreading the meeting. He saw Pilar, still wearing her best clothes, approach the house and stepped outside to meet her. She spoke before he could collect himself.

"Where are Simón and Oskar?"

"They're in town," he said inanely.

Pilar saw that he was under a strain. She examined his face for a clue, but waited for him to speak.

"I'm sad—I'm very sad of what I must tell you, Pilar."

She sank down on a fruit box lying in the grass and waited.

"He was killed yesterday. He is in the mortuary."

"Oh! Ah, the car? The new pickup?"

"Yes, Pilar. He took a pickup to Sandoval's for a drink and had a wreck."

"And now he's dead—Simón," she said calmly, as if she had been expecting it. "Ah—ah, so." She looked off through the trees, then suddenly turned back to John. "And Oskar?"

"No. Oskar still lives. But is broken his leg. He's over in the house of Salinas."

She didn't cry. She thought for a moment. "I must go and see Simón," she said, standing up to go.

"Let me take you to Oskar."

On Tuesday a priest from town buried Simón in a private ranch cemetery. Resourceful Pilar gathered the rest of their cotton with the help of some transient wetbacks, then went back to Mexico with her children.

CHAPTER THREE

Wetback Women

I USED TO THINK THE WETBACKS' SAYING, "El hombre es libre"—"The man is free"—was a joke. It was not; they were perfectly serious about it; their women and children understood it.

Before the revolutions in Mexico, marriage fees were out of reach of the poor. Then the new government nationalized the church property, grounded the bells, dismissed the clergy. As generations had gone by, the people had discovered that ceremonies were not necessary for a happy life. Women were without the protection of the law. I think the wetbacks' mores stemmed largely from centuries of such conditions.

There were many versions and ramifications of "El hombre es libre." It was the man's privilege to carouse all night if he chose; their women understood this, undefended women were fair game. The Mexican border towns all had their oversized boys' towns—red light districts—and many young men are still killed in the Valley in tavern brawls and traffic accidents in the dark early morning hours.

Some changes have come. To get needed records, the government offered civil marriage ceremonies free, and even advertised the service. The poor were slow to take it up, but a few brave ones came, and then more, and then great numbers. The children demanded that papá, mamá, and the grandparents update themselves and get married. I read one news item that told of a ceremony at which fifty couples were married simultaneously; all of their families were there.

Doña Luisa

PUERTAS NUEVAS WAS AN AREA. YEARS ago when the irrigation company replaced the rotten old water-control gates with bright new ones on the big dirt canal that came into the area from the west, people promptly named the place "las puertas nuevas," "the new gates." The canal divided at this point, half flowing north and half continuing east.

A dirt road came up from the south to the canal, then divided to run east and west. It was an important corner, especially for foot or horseback traffic. Foot travelers were funneled by the canals and roads into this corner and used the gate frames for bridges across the canals. An enterprising farmer-gone-broke, Mr. Stone, built a little general store on the road a little way south of the corner and developed a prosperous small business.

The tract of land at the northwest corner of this crossroads had at one time been bought by a northern farmer. He had brought in a shallow well with plentiful, sweet, seepage water and built a three-room house and a broomcorn shed. Then he had failed and had abandoned the place to nature and tax collector. The cleared land had been taken over by second-growth mesquite and cactus.

Other abandoned homes were taken over by wildlife—'possums, rats—or by poor people—squatters needing shelter. The house on the corner had its squatter too. A woman, Doña Luisa, about thirty years old, moved into the little house by the new gates. She needed shelter for herself and her little boy. She might have been widowed, or maybe she had been abandoned by her man. I never heard where she was from. I think she was wet, but she never said so. She worked in the fields, hoeing, stooping, carrying her little boy with her. I began to hear about her from the men who came to my farm seeking work.

"I got something to eat at Doña Luisa's before I came"; "I

stayed at Doña Luisa's last night"; "Doña Luisa fixed a lunch for me." "Doña Luisa" came to be synonymous with "Puertas Nuevas." I gradually gathered that Doña Luisa ran a sort of underground way station on a wetback trail, for lodging, rest, or advice; a hiding place from la chota.

Doña Luisa was quiet but forceful, a motherly person. She must have had some sad experiences, for she had much compassion for all people in trouble. So many newly arrived wetbacks asked for a little something to eat; so many furtive, hungry passers-by stopped at her place, that she had established a business before she knew it—a business known deep into Mexico.

She never seemed to turn anyone away without something: a couple of tortillas, a few leftover beans. If they couldn't pay, she'd say, "When you return, pay me." They must have done so, for she never lacked funds, or credit at Mr. Stone's store.

If they had to stay overnight, the old broomcorn shed, sided up on the north side with paper cartons, was awaiting any number of transients. They slept on the ground on a bunch of grass, possibly as good a bed as some had ever had.

The establishment and all its activities were well hidden behind the weed-grown, high, earth canals, their barrow pits full of water and tule, and the dense-leaved huisaches around on the level ground. It was approached over the water-gate frames by foot or by a tenuous track that came into the yard from the north, down which a ten-gallon can of kerosene was delivered once in a while. No one could possibly enter the area by stealth. The border patrol was always out of luck. At the approach of a motor, or the clamor of the dogs, everyone disappeared into the brush to the east, brush that was still dense native growth, nopal and thorny trees of all kinds.

Doña Luisa was no flirt. Her voice was gentle, her manner smooth. She never hesitated to order a man to bring wood from the adjoining uncleared forty for the deathless bed of live coals in the yard, or a bucket of water from the well, or provisions from the store. It's the only place I ever saw a man grinding *masa* (corn dough) with *metate* and *mano*—stone and hand. A man doesn't have the slapping, marching cadence that a woman evokes from the two stones, but he always got the job done under Doña Luisa's persistent rule.

Anyone in trouble she would harbor or help. Sometimes the men would mention a new girl over there helping Doña Luisa— a girl in trouble, or looking for trouble. Every three or four years Doña Luisa herself would have another child.

She kept her kids clean and busy, their clothes well mended. She sent them to school on a bus that stopped for them on the road across the canal. They seemed to be smart; the last I heard of them, the oldest was in high school.

The dirt canals have been torn down and leveled now, replaced by concrete pipe. The land was resold for taxes. The house and broomcorn shed are gone.

I don't know what happened to gentle-speaking Doña Luisa. Wherever she is, I'll bet those kids are taking care of her. I'll bet she is still concerned with other people's troubles. The Lord surely must have a place reserved especially for Doña Luisa.

Ramona

RAMONA; A PRETTY NAME. SHE WAS slender, erect, well groomed—about sixteen. She kept her head high and carried herself well. She was reserved and poised. She didn't act like a wetback, and her clothes fit. "Mi mamá me showed to sew," she told Lee one time.

Ramona outclassed Renato, that impetuous animal. We

often wondered how the man, off a goat ranch, had gotten tangled up with such a morsel of femininity. He ordered her around, but she didn't jump at his bark. She was slow and fluid in her motions. She fed him on time and always had good midday lunches in a sack for him. We felt that Renato didn't appreciate what he had, but I did hear that she took verbal patches off his hide on occasion.

She was illiterate and would look at writing or print with a total lack of expression. How had an illiterate girl attained such poise and spirit? We couldn't guess—unless she was born that way.

"Renato, how did you get such a pretty girl?" I asked him once.

"Yo la robo," he laughed. "I stole her."

When she became pregnant, Lee found that she'd already had two miscarriages. It helped to explain the look of experience, the womanly poise. We were curious about her.

"How many years had Ramona when you stole her?" I asked Renato later.

"Ramona had eleven years when I her stole."

"Eleven years!"

"Yes, Carlos, I had a struggle to make a woman of her. Batalla mucho!" He didn't elaborate, and I didn't ask again.

She had trouble with her baby. She finally came over and asked Lee what to do. Lee told me that the baby was premature and needed plenty of warmth. She told Ramona what to do, but the girl had no natural instincts for handling babies. She was careless and exposed the baby, and it died.

The men made a little casket in my machine shed, and a cross from a piece of oak. I hauled the coffin and the group of grave diggers to the cemetery in my pickup. It was buried without ceremony. Renato, dry-eyed, tamped the earth and shaped the mound up well.

Ramona later left Renato. She married again and raised a boy in McAllen who grew up and joined the marines and died in Vietnam. They buried him in McAllen with honors.

We wonder sometimes. Has her élan endured?

Rachel

"RAUL?"

"Yes, Carlos?"

"Pablo says he wants to get married; he needs some money."

"He told to me the same."

"But, Raul—he told me that he is going to marry your sister Rachel."

"Yes, Carlos."

"Then it will be a good thing if I lend him the money?" I asked doubtfully.

"Yes, Carlos. I will stand security."

In my self-righteous morality, this came as a shock. It took some thinking.

Raul, my ever-dependable tractor driver, was serious and sober. Pablo was an equally dependable field hand, younger than Raul, who saved his money and didn't carouse.

But Rachel? The less said about her, I would have thought, the better. She visited Raul's family here sometimes. She was big-framed and tall, like her brothers Raul and Efrén. No extra pounds. She was sober, not a flirt. She had a purposeful, breezy walk, and was young and strong. But Rachel was *una puta*, a woman of the night. She lived in the compound outside Reynosa jokingly called boys' town.

Everyone knew it. It was talked about like anything else, with no more emphasis than if she had been a seamstress or a waitress. They all seemed to give her the respect they'd give to any girl, and she looked you straight in the eye when she talked.

How she had come to be in the business, I don't know. I never asked. Maybe a husband had abandoned her and she had gone there of her own accord in order to make a living, or someone in the business had sponsored her. Maybe some man kept her there as a part-time wife, partially supporting her. Maybe someone had stolen her when she was quite young, and she had ended up there in debt.

If she were in debt and a man agreed to pay the debts, he could get her out. I thought probably that was what Pablo intended to do, for he earned enough money so that he should not have needed to borrow for simply a marriage.

I lent him the money. He explained to me in detail how it would be spent: so much for the dress (a white one); so much for underclothing and shoes; so much for drinks; so much for music, and so much for *la corona*—the crown. That was important.

Four Caballeros

THE FOUR BROTHERS WERE NEAR IN AGE, all between twenty-two and thirty. They were tall and well proportioned, although there the resemblance ended; their faces and heads were not the same pattern and their hair ranged from sorrel to black.

One of them worked for Arthur first. He came with a group of people. The next year, he brought two brothers with him, one younger and one older. The following year they brought the youngest one. They were a congenial bunch of boys, but they gradually separated themselves from the herd. They lived and cooked by themselves. They were personally neat and one or more of them must have been good barbers, for they were always well trimmed. You'd sometimes catch one cutting another's hair, although they didn't like to be seen doing this.

Arthur let them have a one-room house, to which they added a tule-roofed *cocina* or "kitchen."

They didn't go back to Mexico often—once every six weeks or so. Arthur thought that was mainly to visit boys' town. Then one time after they came back, he saw a new addition to their establishment—a woman, a girl with a baby. She dodged around the house when she saw Arthur. In the months that followed she always tried to stay out of sight, but gradually Arthur caught enough glimpses of her to assess her points. They were nice.

During the next year or two, the story came out in driblets. She was originally from the mountains south of Mexico City, of mostly Indian blood. She was small and dark, with regular, beautiful features. She had been stolen from her poverty-stricken parents' home when she was quite young, and finally had ended up, in debt, in boys' town. One—or all—of the brothers had fallen for her there. They had dickered with her patrón, paid her debts, and brought her and the baby across the river. She had wanted to come. She seemed to be extremely happy, and she did not seem to favor any one brother over the others.

She established herself as cook—or maybe they'd brought her over with that in mind, for she proceeded to run the house. In time she became more authoritative, ordering the men around to provide fuel, water, and the like. She ordered the groceries, explaining to Arthur just what she wanted from town.

The men seemed to value the female additions to their family and did everything they could for them. They bought the woman pretty clothes and shoes, and she bloomed happily under their attentions. When she had to be gone from the house for a while, or was busy washing, the men entertained the little girl. They made a crib for her and fixed a bouncy hammock on a pole sticking out from the side of the house. They played with her, carried her, tried to teach her to walk, changed her diapers.

"I've never seen wetback men pay a child so much attention," Arthur told me. "The mother came in for her share, too. I oftened wondered what in the background of those brothers had made them so polite and attentive. The wetbacks, as a rule, showed little respect for their womenfolk."

A Family Affair

ALFREDO WAS A CURLY-HAIRED YOUNG wetback who came to my place looking for work. He looked good to me. He seemed intelligent. I had plenty of work, and he made a good man.

He was living in the bunkhouse when Uncle Poppie came over looking for a man who had the makings of a tractor driver. We went over to the bunkhouse that evening and by the light of the kerosene lantern I pointed out Alfredo as the most likely. Uncle Poppie hired him.

Alfredo worked for Uncle Poppie for a couple of years, staying in my bunkhouse. They both were happy. Then one time when Alfredo came back from a visit to Mexico, he had a pretty girl of about twenty-two with him. His wife, he said; a little chunky, but nice. Uncle Poppie let him live in a little stucco-covered house on his place.

Alfredo was a good man, but ambitious. He talked Uncle

Poppie into getting his immigration papers into shape. As almost always happened when a wetback got into this country legally, his feet began to itch. He had to travel. He was no longer a reliable employee; he was fancy free. Wages were higher farther north (as were expenses), and besides, like the others, Alfredo wanted to see the United States. He traveled as far as Washington state on his last trip, going with a truck driver, a small labor contractor.

By this time, Bernardina and Alfredo had two children, the girl still a baby, and Bernardina's cousin, Ruben, thirteen or fourteen and a wetback, was staying with them, working around the area at odd jobs. Alfredo left this little group living in the stucco house. He was regular in sending money orders to Bernardina. She was dressing better than ever, and getting fatter. There were plenty of new clothes for the babies, and I think Bernardina was saving money, for she was a saver where Alfredo was not. After a year and a half in Washington, Alfredo had a chance to come home with a trucker. Just before Alfredo returned, Ruben disappeared.

Alfredo got home, stayed around for a couple of days, and then he too left. Bernardina didn't know where he'd gone, but she didn't seem worried.

Alfredo came back after a week and began to work again. He'd gained knowledge in Washington and now made an excellent hand for Uncle Poppie, for tractor driving and everything else. He stayed home. In a couple of months, another boy was born into the little stucco home. We neighbors thought that Alfredo was certainly taking things in stride. He and Bernardina seemed happy, and after another year came another little girl. Two boys, two girls—a fine family.

Then one time the younger boy, two years old by then, didn't come back with them from a visit to Mexico. Both Alfredo and Bernardina seemed their usual selves.

"Where is little Lázaro?" I asked Bernardina. "I have not seen him since you came back from Mexico."

"Ah, Carlos, him we left in Mexico."

"Was he ill that you left him there?"

"No, Carlos, he has the good health yet, fat as a piglet." She smiled. "Alfredo refused to keep him."

"Sí?"

"Sí, Carlos. One time when he was in Mexico he told my uncle that he would not feed the baby. That when the baby was weaned, he would bring the baby to him. They must care for him."

"You mean that little Lázaro is—"

I started over.

"You mean it was that kid Ruben—" This time I gave up.

Bernardina tilted her head and nodded, smiling. Then at my expression, she giggled. I left.

It must have gotten too cold.

Troubled Woman

AS ED SHUT OFF THE STEAM AND brought the whirling drill stem to a stop, he heard screaming from the chaparral to the north of the drilling rig, a distant, continuing high scream. He looked up at Art, who had stopped in midmotion too. Art waved his arm excitedly toward the path and came down, taking the last dozen feet to the deck in one jump.

"I saw a guy running up the path fast," he yelled at Ed.

"There goes another one, closer in," Ed pointed.

"Should we go after him?"

"We'd better see what's the matter with that woman first."

They ran down the iron stairs and around the slush pit, out into the brush in the direction of the screaming. Behind a bunch of little ebony trees, cradled in a large prickly pear cactus, lay a partially clad woman. She couldn't move at all. She was screaming with pain and fury, mixed with Spanish invective.

"How're we going to get her out?" Ed was yelling now.

"I don't know," Art said, "but first we got to get something to cut with." They shouted at her; she opened her eyes and rolled them wildly. Ed started for an ax at a run. Art began to tear some of the cactus limbs away with a broken mesquite limb, first beating them off with a heavier piece. The woman, or girl—she was small and kind of slender and pretty, what he could see of her—kept screaming. Ed came back with the ax.

"We're going to have to get an ambulance out here," Art told him. "She's got about two million thorns in her." Ed lit out again at a run, this time for the telephone.

Art kept cutting and clearing around the woman so they could get to her. She sped his work with her screams. She was in terrible pain. It was hot and she was facing into the sun. She was glistening with sweat. Art thought, "She ought to pass out. She must be terribly tough. Maybe it's because she's mad."

She'd been picked up bodily and heaved into the middle of the wide old nopal. Her weight had torn some leaves downward and made a nest of thorns for her—sharp, slender thorns with brittle points that broke off easily and stayed in the flesh.

They finally got to her, lifted her out of the cactus, and put her on the ground on her stomach—getting plenty of thorns in their hands and pants in doing it. She moved convulsively once or twice, but it felt better to lie still. She moaned for a while and then changed to yelling vindictive Spanish at them, like a furious cat.

The ambulance came; driver and aide surveyed the problem.

They eased her onto a blanket and with Art and Ed's help carried her out to the ambulance. They left for the hospital with their noisy cargo, leaving Ed and Art feeling deflated.

They shut down the rig, called the sheriff's office, and went back to the scene of the incident. Nearby they found the rest of the woman's scanty clothing. The ground showed marks of a scuffle.

Two sheriff's deputies arrived, looked around and asked a few questions, and decided that it was woman trouble. They said they'd have to talk to the woman herself as a starter, probably the next day when she was out from under the sedatives. They picked up her clothes and a cigarette lighter and left. Ed and Art started drilling operations again.

They went into the sheriff's office a few days later to ask.

"Oh, she's going to be okay. They got some thorns out, got her fever down, wrapped her spiny parts up tight, and turned her over to the border patrol." She had told them the story.

"Mi esposo threw me into the nopal. He picked me up and carried me there, and threw me on top. Tan bárbaro! I kicked, I bit him on the arm."

"Why did he you like that?"

"Because he caught me with Pedro."

"What happened to Pedro?"

"He flew."

"What happened to tu esposo?"

"That knows only God. If ever I see him again, I'll kill him."

"Didn't the border patrol catch either of them?"

"No, they went to the other side fast. But el patrón will give to me the money that they both have earned with him this week."

"You, señora, how do you feel?"

"I feel very good, but muy picada. Much is sticking me. My arms, look! My hands, pobrecitas, my legs, my back, my bottom is full of them broken off. I can't seat myself. And my head, here inside my hair!" They agreed that it was very sad.

"If ever I find aquel Daniel, he'll feel sad too. I'll kill him, el cabrón!"

The deputy told Ed and Art, "She didn't cry or feel sorry for herself."

"She's too pretty to kill anyone," said Ed. "She'll soon forget."

"Yeah, but someone will be easing thorns out of her for a month," Art added. "For a year!"

CHAPTER FOUR

Si
Quiere
Diós

"SI QUIERE DIÓS." "IF GOD WISHES." IT must be accompanied by a small shrug, a resigned, fatalistic little shrug. It implies that, with it, the speaker clears his mind of the matter. It settles arguments. It sums up the situation.

The people came north from their homes in Mexico with no more idea of where they would end up than if they had been locusts. The semiliterate exaggerated their need for a doctor when they were ill. The more primitive ones didn't trust doctors, and generally called only when death was imminent. They all were knowledgeable with native remedies. And no matter what happened, they could shrug and say, "Es como quiere Diós."

"I Want the Doctor"

THE NIGHT WAS COLD. I WAS WARM UNder the quilts. Suddenly I got a jolt in my short ribs from an unfeeling elbow.

"Carrol!"

"What now?"

"Wake up! Someone's knocking at the front door."

I listened. "Are you sure?" I dozed off, and felt more jabs in the ribs.

"Carrol! Get up. See who it is."

"Well, I know what they want," I groaned. I wasn't excited. "Someone just wants the doctor."

"It might be serious, Carrol. Hurry, he'll wake Ingrie. I just got her to sleep again a little while ago."

"All right, I'm going." It was *cold*. "Where the hell are my house shoes?"

"I expect they're where you left them." That was helpful. I felt around under the bed. The floor was cold, too. I found my socks.

It was Raul. Clementina was sick. He wanted someone to take her to the doctor—at two o'clock on a cold, starlit morning with a dry wind blowing from the north.

"But Raul—no is in his office the doctor at this time of the morning."

"No?"

"She was sick all the day—no?" I grumbled, trying not to sound petulant.

"Yes, Carlos, she was sick all the day—yes, very sick."

"Why didn't she go to see the doctor before went down the sun?"

"Because, now, she wishes to."

"Then it is necessary to get up everyone to carry her to the doctor?" Raul was silent against this diatribe. "Like that you all do, in Mexico?"

"No, Carlos," Raul answered patiently, "we don't do that way in Mexico."

"Then why do you do that way here?"

"Because there are many doctors here. They are close. In Mexico we do not have so many cars and pickups, and it is very far to the doctor."

"No can she wait until tomorrow?"

"No, Carlos, very sick she is—muy grave."

"Well, I'll talk to the doctor on the telephone."

I put as much urgency into my voice as Raul had in his, suggesting calamity to the doctor. He told me brusquely to meet him at his office in twenty minutes with the patient. Poor devil; he sounded as if he hadn't even gotten to sleep yet.

Clementina had wrapped a couple of white towels around her head and did look muy grave. Doc said that her malaria had flared up again. Ached? Of course she ached and pained, but . . .

"No, Raul, no can I awaken the druggist at this time of the morning. Clementina will be plenty alive yet when comes out the sun. Then can Lidia carry her to the drugstore for her medicine."

Crying

I STOPPED AND LISTENED. THE SOUND came again. It was not quite like the cry of a mourning dove. It sounded like a sick baby crying half-heartedly, or a baby goat talking to its mother. Some small animal or bird in trouble? It had seemed to come from the direction of the bunkhouse some ninety rods west of our house. Then I didn't hear it.

The next day my youngest boys Mark and Neil and I were still filling the silo by the drainage ditch. I heard the sound again. It was definitely coming from the direction of the bunkhouse. I followed it part way, thinking it could be from one of the roadside ditches near there. As I came nearer, it became more connected and continuous. I decided I'd better run it down and find out what it was when I had a minute.

Later, between loads of silage, I walked down the road toward the bunkhouse, stopping every few steps to listen. Finally I could be sure that it was coming from the bunkhouse itself, or maybe from under it. The kitchen door was open; I came up silently and looked in. The noise was coming from another room whose door also was open. Knowing I was in someone else's house unasked, I went quietly to the door of the room.

A little, gray old man sat on the soiled mattress of a bed, staring at the floor and crying softly in a rising and falling whimper. He was naked except for dirty shorts, and his hair was long and unkempt. He was yellow with sickness. He was in pain; he had been in pain for a long time.

"Buenos días, señor," I said quietly.

He was startled. He focused his eyes on me and smiled, a weak, meaningless smile. But I thought I detected a little pleasure in it.

"Compadre, how is it with you? Are you sick?"

"No——but to me it gives pain here," he said with an effort, slowly extending thin hands on dried-up arms to his lower abdomen. He was in pain such as I'd seldom seen.

I wondered why Leonel, who lived in the bunkhouse, hadn't said anything about him. A proud old Texan whose family was grown, Leonel had left his chattering wife so that he could live in peace; I let him live there, and he worked for me when I needed him. I saw him when he came home at noon that day.

"Who is that over there in your house?" I asked him.

"A man, Carlos. He's wet, the old man."

"But, Leonel, who is he?"

"That, God knows. He was sick. I let him stay here with me."

"Cries he like that all the time?"

"Sí, Carlos, day and night."

"Why don't you do something for him?"

"What can I do for him but to give him some food, when he'll eat it? To me, he said that he has two rich nephews in town. He says they said they have too much family to help him. They threw him out."

"Why don't they take care of him?"

"I don't know, Carlos. I think they have papers to stay here. They may be citizens. To me it seems that they don't want him in their houses finas. He's dirty; he's wet; he stinks."

"What are you going to do with him, Leonel?"

"Give to him food, I think."

"Maybe he'll die on you."

"Quién sabe? Es como quiere Diós."

I went to town and told my doctor about the old man.

"Carrol," the doctor said, "if he's in pain, there are ways of taking care of him. You call Franz Sandell and tell him." I did. Later an ambulance came after him. They took him to the hospital, cleaned him up, gave him a preliminary examination, put some clothes on him, and sent him to Galveston to have some stones removed from his plumbing.

I saw him in the bunkhouse once after he got out of the hospital. I guess he came over to visit Leonel, but maybe to look me up, too. He was cleaned up, shaven, very pale, and still thin, but his bones had taken on a little padding. He fell all over himself thanking me, like a puppy, shaking my hand, hanging on to me. I thought for a little while that he was out of his head. I think maybe the change from continual, hopeless, terrible pain, to no pain, had made him a little punch-drunk.

I felt very foolish that I had not had the wit or curiosity to investigate the noises from the bunkhouse sooner.

Tetanus

ESTEBAN HAD FORTITUDE. HE STOOD ON
my step, slender and erect, and the only sign of the strain he
was under was his unshaven jaw twitching his cud of Lobo
Negro a little faster than usual. He had crossed the river at
Granjeno and come sixteen miles, to be ringing our patio bell
at about 11:30 A.M. I didn't ask him how.

"So serious, Esteban? Such a calamity!"

"Sí, Don Carlos."

"That a thing so ugly can happen to your son Miguel!
Where did he catch it, the tetanus?"

"God might understand, Carlos," said the old man, shrug-
ging his shoulders.

"Excuse me while I change my clothes. We will take the
pickup, pass through Edinburg for some money, and arrive at
the hospital fast."

Several days earlier Miguel, working for me, had started
feeling too sick to work. I had taken him to an American contract doctor in Edinburg. I don't remember exactly what the
doctor had said, but he had dismissed Miguel with a prescrip-
tion, and I had gathered that Miguel was coming down with a
virulent case of flu. On the way home, Miguel had been unhappy about the diagnosis, and in the afternoon he had told
me he was going home with a friend. "Está ignorante aquel
doctor! I have something more worse than a cold," he had
said with conviction. "Better the médicos mejicanos." I had
disagreed with him and told him so, but he had been adamant.
Three days later his anxious father was ringing our patio bell.
Miguel was in a hospital in Reynosa.

"He needs muchos inyecciones. The money has quit; the
money borrowed from the relatives has quit too." Two farma-

cias had run out of the medicine, and the third would not let them have any more without cash.

We drove up to the uninspiring brick house that served as hospital, and hurried through the gate, up the aged flagstone walk to the porch where Miguel's brothers Antonio and Francisco and his uncles Fidel, Neto, and Carlos were waiting. We all went quickly into the office, a room off the central hall with old plastered walls and cracked, thick masonry. The young doctor sat in an ancient swivel chair, his feet up on an equally ancient desk, waiting.

"Is this thing true that Miguel has tetanus?" I asked.

"Sí, señor."

"How many dolares are necessary for the medicine at this time?"

"Fifty at once. After these injections are finished, who knows?"

I counted off fifty dollars and handed the money to Esteban, who scooted out the door before I could speak. Antonio touched my elbow.

"Might Don Carlos like to see him?"

"Yes, Antonio, cómo no?" I glanced at the doctor. He nodded. We went through the hall into another bare room with cracked walls. On a white iron bed with chipped enamel, lay Miguel, twisting wildly with pain on the soiled bare mattress. Chilo and Lorenzo, sweating, were holding him mightily to the bed. It was midday hot inside the room, and still. In shorts only, Miguel was drenched with big beads of sweat. Hiliberto Gómez fluttered around with a towel, wiping the sweat from Miguel's body when he could. They all nodded to me, and Antonio leaned over the bed and spoke to Miguel's closed eyes.

"Here's Carlos—Carlos has arrived."

Miguel continued to strain against his holders, his muscles

bulging, but he opened his eyes and whisked them around, searching. They came to rest on me. His jaws were clamped. The convulsive struggles didn't lessen, but his eyes, terribly expressive, stayed on me. His face was covered with a heavy black beard. I was startled that he was rational. The men were surprised, too; they said it was for but an instant.

We waited for Esteban to come back with the medicine. There was low, intermittent talk among the watchers. I decided to speak.

"Miguel, this is Carlos. How goes it with you? It's sorry I am to see you like this." What the hell do you say to a man who's in mortal agony, I asked myself. "But you are going to be all right—have no fear. You have a good doctor. Hurry up! The work is waiting." I gave up. It was no use trying to get through to him. I turned to Antonio.

"Know you what happened to your papá?" He nodded.

"He went to the farmacia."

Francisco and I went to look for Esteban, hoping to save time. We missed him at two pharmacies, but picked him up on the way back to the hospital. He was trotting, carrying a glass jar in a paper sack, carefully. The doctor had his tools out on the table, his shirt off, and two of the men ready to help him.

I looked in on Miguel before I left. Lorenzo and Chilo were holding him down again. The men had been taking turns holding him twenty-four hours a day.

"Esteban, should I leave more money with you?"

"No, Carlos, no—not at this time. If it is necessary, I will send Francisco for it."

"Miguel knew me when I entered," I told Esteban, hoping to encourage him.

"He did! Thanks to God. Then he is bettering himself."

"I think he will get well."

"It is as God wishes."

About two months later, Miguel showed up for work—sunburned again, but not yet completely fleshened up.

"What do you think of this thing, Miguel? Where did it catch you?"

"I don't know, Carlos, except that when I irrigated that last turno [shift] in the pasture, I had only one sock on. The other boot galled my bare ankle. I can think of nothing else. But Carlos," he added, "when to me you spoke there in the hospital, I heard what you said."

"Truly, Miguel?"

"Sí, I understood every word. And where is it, the work that is waiting?"

Polo

LEOPOLDO WAS A SLIM YOUNG WETback. I used him mainly to irrigate. He was from an irrigation district in Torreon where only oversized hoes were used to guide the water; to build dams across field laterals instead of *lonas* (cloth dams); to build canals and field laterals. He was good.

He was an expert at hitting things he threw at. He often came past the house at quitting time carrying a newly killed jackrabbit or cottontail, having thrown something at it—a wrench, a stick, a piece of mesquite or ebony root, a clod—and stunned or killed it. Once when his shovel was stuck in the muddy canal bank fifty feet from where he was standing, a blackbird alighted on the top end of the handle. He picked up a clod and threw. The bird flew before the clod hit, but the clod pulverized right on the end of the handle. I'd never seen such accuracy anywhere.

Polo wanted to marry the daughter of the family with whom he had been staying, squatters on some vacant lots over in the northwest part of town in a half-tent, half-board house. He came to me.

"How much money do you need, Polo?"

"I will need twenty-five dollars to buy la ropa [the clothes] for Angelita." I lent him the money. I was invited to the wedding, but didn't go. The morning after, Polo came to work a little early—at 6:30.

"What are you doing here so early, Polo?" I asked in surprise.

"Está mala, Angelita. Por favor, Carlos, I want you to bring a doctor."

"This is too early to find a doctor, Polo, but if she is very sick I will go as soon as I get my milking done."

"All right, Carlos. You may be sure that she needs a doctor much and soon!"

What had Polo done? His wedding night—and she needed a doctor bad! It was hard for me to believe that I was rolling down the road in my Model T on such a fool's errand.

I found Dr. Paul in his office and explained the situation to him. He couldn't understand what that Mexican had done to his bride on his wedding night, either, but the call for help hurried him. Rather than try to explain how to find the house, I took him.

Polo was standing outside with his father-in-law. Both looked relieved when we drove up. They ushered the doctor into the shack.

He was inside for about fifteen minutes, then came out laughing. He wasn't carrying his bag. He came over to the car and put his foot up on the running board to get confidential.

"That little girl is going to have a baby!"

"How soon?"

"It's on its way."

"Are you going to wait?"

"Yes, Carrol, I don't think I'd get back to the office before it comes."

The baby came soon. In about a half-hour I drove old Doc back to his office. He was grave and worried.

"I'll have to get my car and come back in a little while," he told me. "That girl is sick. Fever."

Polo didn't come the next day, but the day after that he came and told me that Angelita was dead. He had to make arrangements to bury her; he needed a little more money. I heard later that she was buried in her bridal garments.

Her parents raised the little boy, and he thrived. For a while Polo kept working for me and living with his in-laws. In a few years I lost track of them; they drifted off to the north.

Gabrielito

ONE SPRING MORNING A LONG, SLIGHTLY bowlegged, light-complexioned Mexican with green eyes was waiting for me in my barn. He wanted work. I talked with him. Something about his quick responses and alertness made me think he might not make an industrious field hand—that he probably had the potential for a troublemaker. But I needed hands, so I put him to work anyway.

I decided later to develop Gabriel into a tractor driver because of the continual interest he showed in my tractors and machinery and the knowledge he had picked up somewhere of engines. He shaped up nicely. In a couple of years, I could trust him with any of my tractor work. Three of his younger brothers later worked for me steadily for many years as tractor drivers.

Eventually Gabriel brought his tall, husky young wife over to cook for them. They lived in a tenant house I had down the road. It was here that Gabrielito was born. Gabriel and Josefa had him registered and baptized as a United States citizen.

"Now you have a little Americano," I said to his papa after the ceremony. "How does it seem to have a son who is an American?"

"Very good, Carlos. He can grow up here and go to school here. La chota cannot be so strong with us when they catch us, for our babito has American birth papers. They will protect us."

"That's sure. They won't put a person carrying American birth papers across the Rio Grande. That is against the law. He's here to stay, Gabriel, no?"

"Sí, Carlos, that is true."

Then Gabriel began spitting blood in small quantities. I worried; I spoke to him several times about it.

"Gabriel, why spit you blood so much? You'd better go to see a doctor."

"I don't know, Carlos. It doesn't give me pain anywhere."

"You should see a doctor, Gabriel. I'll take you."

"No, doctors are not too wise. I think I'll not go." He didn't seem worried. He went on working. I talked to Josefa.

"No, Carlos. Always Gabriel does as Gabriel wishes. It is sad, Carlos, but es como quiere Diós."

Then Gabriel failed to come back from a visit to Mexico. Jesus, his youngest brother, told me Gabriel was feeling weak. Later Jesus told me that Gabriel was sick, and at last that his brother was dead. Tuberculosis had taken him.

Gabriel's comely widow sometimes visited his brothers over here for the day, perhaps to bring a message. She'd have Gabrielito in tow. She doted on him, her little Americano.

"Are you going to send Gabrielito to school here, Josefa?" I asked her on one visit.

"That knows only God, and He has not told me. I wish so, but I must live on the other side. So wanted Gabriel too. Who knows?" she answered, snuggling Gabrielito. He had come to her crying and she had stood him up on a table in the patio, the better to quiet him. During our talk she had been cuddling him and massaging his penis through his thin pants, visibly soothing his rumpled feelings.

"If I could find work for all the time here . . . But I'm trained for nothing but to work outside in the fields."

For Josefa, Gabrielito's birth certificate was a pass through border customs, across the bridge, although the boy never went to school here. But Josefa was strict about his duties as an American citizen, so for the Vietnam war Gabriel Junior did not wait to be drafted. He enlisted.

They brought him back in a flag-draped casket with an honor guard. He had spent very little of his life in the United States, where he is buried as an American soldier.

T.B.

ANDRÉS, TWO YEARS YOUNGER THAN HIS brother Gabriel, was one of my tractor drivers for years as a wetback. Then the bracero program came into effect. In order to get our men we had to follow certain rules: We filled out applications and went, at a specified time, to pick up the men at the bridge; there were physical examinations, pictures to be taken, contracts to sign, insurance to buy.

When I tried to hire Andrés as a bracero, he was turned

back after the physical examination—because of tuberculosis. Although Gabriel had died of the disease, I couldn't believe that wiry, tough Andrés was a sick man.

"He's in the last stages of T.B.," reported a friend whom I had asked to double-check the health records when I heard the news. "The doctor showed me the negatives. Doc says he won't be alive in six months; his lungs are shot to pieces."

Andrés was thin, but then he'd always been the thinnest of the brothers. He had a good healthy sunburn. He seemed to have all his strength. I still believed they had crossed his negatives with someone else's.

He'd married little Felicita, sixteen, who had been born on our place. They had two babies. Felicita was a U.S. citizen and so were her children; now Andrés would have to stay in Mexico, and they with him, or he'd have to keep coming over wet. I'd lent him three hundred dollars to buy a car; the car would now stand down there in Mexico and rust.

"It's bad, Carlos. I can't pay unless I work for you. It needs gas, too, and I can't buy gas unless I work for you. No money, no gas." His logic was sound. He laughed about the tuberculosis.

"No got me T.B., Carlos. Gabriel died, but me no. Look," he flexed a wiry arm, "soy fuerte; I'm strong."

But the border patrol had more men, better educated and better trained, with more sophisticated equipment. They were thinning out the wetbacks in the Valley. Andrés was stuck in Mexico, and Felicita and the children with him. I was stuck with losing a tractor driver and three hundred dollars.

Five years later Andrés drove into my yard in a saggy-rear-end car full of kids. His Felicita, fatter and smiling, jumped out and almost hugged me. Andrés came around and gave me a powerful abrazo. His grip was firm. He tossed his cornshuck cigarette butt to the ground, stepped on it, and spat.

"Ah, qué, Andrés, I thought that dead you were!"

"No, Carlos. Yet, I'm not dead. Maybe later, yes," he grinned with his small, tobacco-stained teeth.

"Por qué, Andres?—why are you not dead?"

"Who knows? Perhaps it is a thing of God. With health I'm very good. The pocket, it's another thing."

He had fattened up some, but not much. He was as sunburned as ever.

"You went to the doctor, Andrés?"

"No," he laughed as if to say, "How foolish," and shrugged his shoulders Mexican-style.

"Have you quit the coughing?"

"Yes, Carlos, hardly ever."

"How many kids you got there?"

Felicita spoke for him. "Six."

"It's working all right, then, all your body, Andrés?"

"Yes, Carlos, I feel fine, muy bien."

When he drove into the yard ten years later he had ten kids, some of them with him in a pickup. Well-fed Felicita was fatter than ever.

CHAPTER FIVE

Bandidos
on
Both Sides

THE RIO GRANDE IS THE RIO BRAVO—
Wild River—to the Mexicans. Before it was tamed by the
thirty-four dams on its watershed it commanded respect, and
to people in trouble the other side always looked better. Mexican refugees, Texas outlaws, eastern thugs, generations of cattle
rustlers, horse-stealing Indians, Pancho Villas have traded and
raided and run back and forth across the line for centuries.

They had nothing on the present-day Mexican bandidos:
gleaners, scavengers—hungry people, who, if they couldn't
bargain for what they needed, didn't have the means to trade
for it, would take it. But mostly they worked, and carried off
their booty in the form of negotiable money.

Border Thievery

FELIPE AND MANUEL, A PAIR OF YOUNG
Texans—farm boys and friends—wanted to farm. Manuel's
people had a few hundred acres of land on the river above
Quevitas. The boys rented a hundred and twenty-five acres of
the land from the old folks for a quarter-crop rent.

Farming was their life's ambition, but it was expensive to start. First, they needed drinking water on the place. They rigged their equipment and bored, finding sweet water in the fourth location—a real flow. Their well-drilling equipment was stolen that night by kibitzers who had been crossing the river to watch them drill.

Their first harvest-to-be was beans. A thirteen-inch rain on the arroyo up by Rio Grande City came down the Rio Grande. The water backed up and over the bean field, destroying all but seventeen rows. Felipe and Manuel picked 2,500 pounds of beans—but at least that much disappeared at night.

The next crop to mature was their corn, twenty acres. They sold a few roasting ears and left the rest to dry. When they went to gather it, they found the field hollow inside. Only a strip of corn around the edge of the field had been left un-picked for show; the rest had already been gathered, nubbins and all. A conservative guess was that seven hundred bushels swam the river.

They had forty acres of fine potatoes on higher ground, which escaped the flood. On periodic inspections, they found that others had been inspecting, too—pulling up plants here and there to see how the young potatoes were developing.

While Felipe and Manuel were preparing the potato digger for the harvest, wetbacks came over every day asking for work. Finally Manuel announced, "Tomorrow we will start the machine, but we will need only fifteen helpers to begin with."

Tomorrow came—also a hundred people. Manuel picked fifteen and told the rest to go home, but they stood around watching. Each had his *morral* (a kind of shoulder knapsack) to carry odds and ends and his noon lunch in; most Mexicans have them. Potatoes were disappearing right there in the field while the owners tinkered with their machine.

The field was close by a brush-filled arroyo. Felipe and Manuel checked the brush and found that the wetbacks had been emptying their potato-filled morrales into larger sacks. So they made everyone except the fifteen helpers leave the field. The people went no farther than the arroyo and hovered there in the shade.

The harvest went well; the wastage was big. Felipe and Manuel had to run the extra people off time after time. They told them there would be plenty of potatoes for all after the machine had gone over the ground.

"Go home until we get through harvesting. Then you can have the field."

The potato market fell when they were one-third through the harvest. After several weeks the market still had not recovered, so Felipe and Manuel told the people to help themselves. The following morning hundreds of people from across the river flocked to the field. In two days the potatoes were gone. The ground had been searched to a depth of eighteen inches, every kind of tool used for digging.

Felipe and Manuel had lost heavily on the year's venture, but they were curious. They crossed to Mexico on the ferry at Los Ébanos to scout the *fruterías* and stores. They found their potatoes everywhere in the little river towns, nice and clean but not sorted. They found their neighbor's big red tomatoes, too. The merchants said they had bought the tomatoes from a trucker who told them they were from the state of Sinaloa.

All the produce had been taken across the river by swimmers. Felipe and Manual could find no evidence that anyone had used a boat. Their conservative estimate was that 2,500 pounds of pinto beans had gone across, 22 tons of corn, 100 tons of potatoes, and 15 tons of tomatoes.

The river was full of swimmers.

Poker Winnings

ARTURO WORKED FOR PAT, AN ACTIVE ginner, during the summer months. His regular work the rest of the year was with a citrus packing plant down the siding a few blocks.

Very few people knew that Arturo was a wetback. He passed everywhere for a U.S. citizen. He earned good money and dressed fashionably, even if maybe he overdid the amounts of sweet odors he sprayed on himself. He spoke enough English to discuss anything, never reverting to Spanish.

Pat liked him. Arturo was versatile, intelligent, quick. Pat put him to work where these things counted. He depended on Arturo, and sent him on confidential errands. Pat himself didn't like to be tied down too closely with detail.

"Arturo," he told his helper one afternoon, "if Frances calls and I'm not here, tell her I won't be home for supper. A couple of buyers will be here and I'll most likely be late." Pat left the office with some bale listings to check out in the yard. He was feeling expansive. He'd replenished the supply of beer in the cooler back in his very private office. He had a semi-understanding with one of the buyers, and a couple of his town cronies were coming for a poker game that night. Pat kept Arturo in attendance at such festivities, and, as the ginning season was closing, he expected not to be disturbed for the evening.

Pat was a big blustery guy. He liked company, liked to entertain, to talk of hunting and guns and things like that that really count. He was good in business, good at big deals, and he carried a large wad of money. At the poker games he never had too much cash on him, though. If luck was against him and he went broke, he'd quit. "I'm out of money, boys. Sorry. See you next time. Have another beer." But if a guest broke, it was, "That's all right. How much do you need? Let's keep going!" He'd send Arturo out to the depository in his car for the necessary amount. Arturo was used to being sent on such intimate affairs.

This night, Pat was unusually jovial. He drank more than the rest, but his luck was holding. Arturo was sent many times out to the car to replenish the disappearing stakes of Pat's friends (or to add Pat's winnings to the money in the box). Some hundred-dollar bills were flowing. Everyone was loudly happy, until Arturo failed to return from an errand to the car.

"I wonder what's the matter with Arturo," Pat said, and then forgot his anxiety in being the congenial host. His companions pressed him.

"You'd better go see about Arturo." They had already borrowed too much from Pat to keep the game going.

Pat finally went. The gin yard was lighted up. He didn't see Arturo. He went over to his big black car. The depository was gone!

"I wonder if someone knocked Arturo in the head," he worried. There was no use in calling the police; he realized he was too foggy to think well. The game broke up.

In the morning Arturo was still gone. There was no sign of a scuffle. Still, it was nothing to report to the police. Pat went to his citrus packing friend.

"You told me Arturo was absolutely trustworthy."

"Well, I've employed him for twelve years. Don't worry, Pat, he'll show up!"

"But there was over nine hundred dollars in that box, as nearly as I can figure."

As time went on, these two practical businessmen reluctantly decided that the large amount of money, and the freedom and carelessness with which it was being handled, had been too much for Arturo; that he had left for Mexico with the whole roll.

No one here has seen him since.

Voting

ENRIQUE AND CHONO WERE TWO OF MY steady hands in the late twenties. They were wetbacks, but didn't go home very often to visit; they stayed whether or not I had work for them, so I let them use a fairly good one-room house as a permanent arrangement. They kept to themselves and were inconspicuous. By instinct or plan, they never were picked up by the border patrol. Possibly it was because they adapted easily to American ways and mannerisms. No one would have suspected them of being wetbacks.

When Enrique began to act a little standoffish, a little guilty, toward me, it bothered me. I liked the fellows. I wondered if they intended to pull a fast one. I was not unfamiliar with the signs.

"Enrique is getting a little surly," I told Lee one day. "It's growing on him—Chono, too, I think."

"What do they have to feel like that about?" she asked.

"I don't know, but it seems like Enrique has a chip on his shoulder."

Enrique's abrasiveness never got bad enough so that I could ask him about it. I hoped it would blow over. Then he came to me one evening.

"I think that me and Chono won't come to work tomorrow. We have business there in Edinburgo."

"You're going to be all day over there?" I asked.

"Yes, Carlos, but we return before Wednesday."

"Very well, Enrique. But the inspectors are getting a little mad at me for not getting out those few cotton stalks that are left."

"Yes, Carlos, we know, but we have this little business."

The next day was election day. It was a hot election. We were trying to throw the old ring out, a corrupt white estab-

lishment that for many years had sucked white the living substance of the county.

There was a crowd in line when I went to vote—and there
stood my Enrique and Chono, patiently waiting. They ignored
me, very stolidly failed to see me. So that was what had been
bothering them! They didn't come home that evening, but
they came to work the next day and thereafter. They acted the
way my kids did when they'd done something out of line. I
ignored it until days later, when everything was smooth.

"I saw you boys at the voting last Tuesday," I remarked.

"Yes, Carlos, we went up and voted," Enrique answered.

"How did you vote?" I was curious to see if they understood
what they had done, and if they would tell me.

"Well, we—ah—they told us not to advise el patrón on
that business. But—ah—we voted the democrático, like the
man told us to, derecho"—straight.

"What man?" I wanted to know.

"In the spring a man came to my house and asked if we
wanted to vote. I said, 'Yes, but we have never voted.' "

"He came out here?"

"Yes, Carlos. He asked our names, Chono and me, and said
he would be back."

"Well, did he come back?"

"Yes, Carlos, he gave us each a little piece of paper and
told us to keep it until we voted, and two dolares! 'After you
vote,' he said, 'I'll give you each two more.' He told us not
to pay any attention to el patrón, Carlos."

"Did he give you those two dollars, the last ones?"

"Yes, Carlos, and he showed us how to vote."

"Sí?"

"Sí, before the voting, he told us to come to an old store
building in town. There were others there also."

"Were the others mojados, like yourselves?"

"I don't know, Carlos. I think so. I think some were from

here, also. We learned how to vote. They had long papers, like a newspaper with lists down the long way—like this. The thing was, we left the first column. We were not to mark in it, not do anything with the first list on the left side of the paper. But we were to make lines through all of the others.

"It is easy, Carlos, to vote. Everyone should vote. It is a thing very good that a man should vote."

Changing Fields

CHARLES HAD A PIECE OF LUCK ONE morning. A cotton picking crew came by, a big crew, in two trucks.

"Do you have some good cotton to pick?" asked the crew chief.

"Yes, I have a field down the road that's never been picked over."

"How big?"

"Twenty acres."

"Let's go and see it."

Several of the men climbed in Charles's pickup and they went to inspect the field. They were satisfied with it, and, as the price of a first picking had standardized in the community, there was no dickering. The trucks moved down and thirty hands strung out across the field.

Charles went home to breakfast, feeling good. He ate with relish, lighted a cigarette, and talked to his wife for a while. Then he went out to see how the hands were doing.

They weren't there. They had left, with the cotton they had picked lying abandoned in a little pile at the end of the field. Charles had a sinking feeling in the pit of his stomach. It had happened again. Irresponsible people! Next year, he was going to get a cotton picker; a machine. But where had they gone?

Before he started his pickup, he climbed up into its bed to look around. There was activity down at the end of his neighbor's field. He went to look. Same trucks, same drivers. Louie had pulled a fast one on him again—stolen his crew.

Charles walked over to the drivers. They didn't want to talk to him, but he cornered them. "Why are you picking over here?"

"El dueño came over and told us he had much better picking over here, and to us it seemed so, so we moved our people over here." While Charles was talking to the drivers, a few of the hands came out of the field. They seemed unhappy.

"This cotton is hard to pick," one said. "The cotton sticks in the casquillos too hard and the points are sharp. It is hard on the fingers, and not all of the locks come out."

"What can be done?" asked one of the drivers.

"We think it is best that we go back to the cotton of this patrón. It had bigger locks." The drivers were at the mercy of the crew. They seemed to be in favor of going back.

"NO," Charles said. "You people have the crooked tongue. It is better for you to stay here and pick for el señor Louie. He has a foul tongue too. You are good compadres to each other—you and him. I think that he talks even more crooked than you."

"Yes, pero, señor—"

"I can't think of anything better for you than to have el señor Louie for your patrón."

"Pero, patrón, don't anger yourself at us."

"Señor Louie will teach you things about lying that you never knew."

Haughty

AT ONE TIME I WAS COMMUNITY COM-
mitteeman for the emergency farm program. One of my duties
was to measure the acreages of field crops on each farm. We
used a surveyor's chain (sixty-six feet long). The farm owner
or his representative had to carry one end of the chain to en-
sure that no mistakes in field boundaries were made.

Mr. Gómez was of Mexican descent. A revolution had run
his people out of Mexico a generation or two earlier. He and
his father before him were successful businessmen. They had
big cars and wide bottoms. Mr. Gómez owned a large acreage
in the dry lands and had a government crop contract as a
farmer. Farmed for fun, I guess, with hired help.

We went to his farm in the early morning in his car. We
disembarked, strung out the chain, and proceeded up one of
his field roads, measuring. Mr. Gómez took the lead end of
the chain and placed the iron stakes; I followed carrying the
rear end and picking up the stakes. Up one sandy field-road
and down another we went. The sun was bright.

Mr. Gómez got hot. His striped shirt got soaked with sweat.
He was thirsty. We passed a ten-gallon water can at the end of
the cotton rows, put there for the pickers. The child of one
wetback picker was getting a drink, using a wire-handled tomato can for a dipper—a little boy of about ten with scanty
clothing and no shoes.

Mr. Gómez passed him and the can at an even stride. Without looking up, he told the boy to give him a drink. The boy
loosed his short tow picking-sack from his slender waist,
dropped it to the ground, and struggled to get the lid back off
the can. Following the dragging chain, I'd passed him by this
time. He finally got the lid off, filled the drinking cup, and

came trotting behind me, trying to catch up with Mr. Gómez without spilling the water.

By the time the boy caught Mr. Gómez, we had measured three lengths of the chain. He called to Mr. Gómez. Mr. Gómez kept going until the chain was taut, set the stake, took the cup, drank the water, and handed the cup back to the boy—still without looking at him. Without a word of thanks Mr. Gómez started off again down the road, dragging the light chain. The boy trotted back to the watering can through the hot red dust and refastened his soiled tow-sack around his middle. Mr. Gómez waddled on, and I kept following, gathering up counting stakes.

Paid in Full

BOB SURVEYED THE LITTLE GROUP OF anxious wetbacks in his yard. They looked like responsible people to him. "I have but very little cotton—not much work for you," he told them. They seemed to understand.

"It makes no difference. Can we stay here and work afuera— outside?" They looked around the farmyard, especially at Bob's old horse barn.

"If you want to, you can live in that old barn, you are welcome," Bob offered, gesturing toward the long-unused barn. "You can stay there and look for work around here. There's a well over there. The water is sweet. I'll find you a bucket. Understand?"

"That's very good, señor," said one. To the others he pointed out, "This place is well hidden." "This is all right," they agreed. They gathered up some old utensils from the tin can pile. Bob brought them others discarded from the farm kitchen. They found some broken concrete blocks for a fireplace and an old disk blade for an oven, and they were established.

They were happy and cheerful. They had a patrón muy simpático, an excellent place to sleep that would keep the dews off; they were well hidden and off the main roads. They stayed around until Bob had some cotton chopping to do. This finished, they looked industriously for other work. A neighbor a mile to the south—a cattleman—needed four hands for a few days. Bob didn't like the big-hatted man who always had a sad-looking cigarette stuck to his lips when he talked, but thought it would be all right for the men to work for him.

Mr. Richards's work lasted three or four days. He anticipated the time when the men would finish and had the border patrol there to pick them up. He refused to pay them. The patrolmen had no authority to force him; they had caught a cargo of wetbacks, so they left with them. All four were back at Bob's within twenty-four hours. They refused to go back to work for Mr. Richards.

"That cabrón paid us not one cent. 'tá muy cabrón, him. Very wild. We don't work with him more." They shook their heads angrily.

"Well," Bob nodded, "if you don't wish to, then, that's the way it is. But I don't have any work for you, not until cotton picking."

"We will in some manner get along." They did get along, but Bob saw to it that they had enough food. In about a month, Mr. Richards came looking for help again. The men needed the work, but they wouldn't go. Mr. Richards got mad, got in his battered old pickup, and left. Before dinner, la chota was out at Bob's with a paddy wagon and picked up all eight men. In a few days they were all back again, and comfortably busy around the neighborhood with various farmers. Again la chota descended and took them all one night. Mr. Richards, up to the same trick. His reason? He had a good one and didn't mind expressing it.

"These wetbacks don't belong over here! If everybody would report them to la chota, they'd stay home." It was unassailable, except he never did say why he had tried to hire them himself.

They were back in a week. They picked Bob's cotton without being picked up again, then went home, refusing to pick for anyone else.

In the fall, when Mr. Richards was shredding his cotton stalks, a blade of the shredder flew off and mangled his foot and ankle. He was permanently crippled. Bob said, "He deserved it for cheating those poor wetbacks. There's no telling how many other wetbacks he did the same thing to."

A Foreman

SOME VALLEY FARMERS' OPERATIONS were large enough to require a foreman; other farmers just thought their operations were large enough. It was a matter of status that allowed the owner the freedom and time to be sociable with other operators. They gathered at the coffee counters and talked shop.

Arthur Thompson's foreman was American-born and Spanish-speaking. He was a great help, augmenting Arthur's meager Spanish. Arthur let Federico handle all matters concerning the men: their numbers, food, quarters, and pay. Federico had a spot all his own on the bank of the Rio Grande. When he needed a hand, or twenty-five hands, he'd go down and whistle shrilly, then wait in the shade of the jara for someone to come bobbing across in a lancha. Federico would tell him what he wanted: so many men, or certain individuals, to come to work, when and for how long. The people soon would show up at the Thompson place.

Federico had a helper, a bookkeeper, Alfredo. Fat and wide, Alfredo also was a U.S. citizen, and he knew his way around.

Arthur explained his requirements to Federico and stated how much he would pay for the work, Federico dealt with the men, and Alfredo kept the books. It was efficient for Arthur.

By the amounts of money that Federico and Alfredo always had available to spend on their families, Arthur knew that the two were somehow cheating the men. He investigated. He found that a wetback who had forty or fifty dollars coming to him was getting only ten or fifteen dollars take-home pay. Arthur was paying the stated amount, Federico was paying the men less, and Alfredo was falsifying the accounts. For example, Federico charged each man two dollars for a trip to town, and kept out a commission on their grocery and clothing bills.

Arthur didn't like it, but he decided that he was free from guilt; *he* wasn't robbing the men. He was paying a fair, stipulated price. Federico, with Alfredo's help, was doing the stealing. It was a "family affair" (all Mexicans).

Arthur told himself that as long as he was getting his work done, he had no complaint. It was no business of his what his American help was paying their cousins from across the river.

The Drunkard

"IT IS BETTER THAT I GO HOME, CAR-
los," said Lorenzo at noon.

"How long did you irrigate this time? Two and a half days
and two nights, no? Fifty-four hours?"

"Yes, Carlos, and I haven't been to the other side for three
weeks. I wish to see mi mamá. She might have need of some
money."

"I think you had better go, Lorenzo. Do you want to leave
Edinburg by the bus? Or shall I take you to McAllen for the
Reynosa bus?"

"Edinburgo. I wish to buy some things in the stores there."

Lorenzo was very tired. We bought his things. I settled up
with him, and he had eighty or ninety dollars. I saw him buy
his ticket and left him sitting on the blue bench in front of
the bus station, surrounded by his things. It was three weeks
before I saw him again. He came trailing in one morning
freshly shaven, with his hair trimmed and new work clothes
on.

"Good day, Lorenzo. Where have you been?"

"I stayed at the ranch, Carlos. I was very tired. I thought
it better if I rested a little and besides, mi papá needed that I
help to cut the corn fodder."

Lorenzo went right to work, but he seemed to have something on his mind. I waited, and when he got ready to tell me,
it came.

"Remember you, Carlos, the day you took me to the bus
station?"

"Yes, Lorenzo, why?"

"The police arrested me that day."

"Here in Edinburg?" He nodded with hurt eyes. "And why
did they arrest you, Lorenzo?"

"They arrested me for being drunk. A man with a gun and blue clothes arrested me by that bench in the bus station."

"You weren't drunk, Lorenzo!"

"I was asleep on the bench, very much asleep. This policía said I was drunk."

"The old cabrón, what did he do?"

"He took me to the house of the police."

"Did they put you in jail? Or did you have to pay a fine?"

"I paid the fine—ten dollars, Carlos. I wasn't drunk. I was very, very sleepy. I hadn't slept for two nights—remember?"

"Yes, I remember. What then?"

"They let me go. I had to walk back to the bus station, carrying my purchases, too. Cabrones, no?"

"Cabrones, no, Lorenzo, bandidos, sí. I wish that I had known about it."

"Yes, but now it's very late, no?"

"Yes, it is late for a poor man. You should have told me as soon as possible. Now it's three weeks pasado."

"Yes," he answered reflectively—thinking of the ten dollars.

"Was he a Mexican? The policeman?"

"Yes, puro mejicano."

I thought of the ten dollars too. Totally unjust. A Mexican-American policeman taking something-or-other out on a poor Mexican.

"Well, Lorenzo, it seems to me that it does no good to think about trying to correct this foul thing now. They would just deny it. And too, they might get ugly and report you to la chota."

"Yes, Carlos, to me also it like that seems."

CHAPTER SIX

La
Chota

IN 1922 I CAME FROM CENTRAL KANSAS
to south Texas riding in an immigrant railroad car that contained our household goods, farm machinery, and two teams of mule colts. The railroad required a caretaker with each car transporting animals.

The long, disastrous nationwide railroad strike was in progress. Railroad equipment was deteriorating and worn out; overloaded engines gasped and faltered and stopped. The trip, only two or three days in normal times, had taken nine days.

The tired engine stopped the train to switch in Raymondville. I clambered down from the fenced-up door of the boxcar that had been my home for more than a week. From my perch atop this board fence, I had seen the sign of an eating place across the street, a half-block away.

I was hungry, filthy, unshaven. I angled over toward the sign. As I started to cross, a Model T Ford with two uniformed men in the front seat stopped in the middle of the wide, dusty street. The men wore flat-brimmed felt hats, khaki shirts and pants, and high-heeled boots. The nearer man motioned me over to him.

I went. I was curious. It was strange country to me, with strange ways; even the weeds were strange. I had thought Texas Rangers rode alone; that it took only one? They looked me over as I came.

"Where're you from, boy?"

"I'm from Kansas."

The officer seemed surprised. He took a closer look at me. He hadn't expected me to speak English, I decided later.

"Where're you going?"

I pointed. "Over there to get me something to eat. Why?"

"We just wanted to know. He shoved in the clutch and the jitney started to move.

"Are you Texas Rangers?" I asked quickly.

"Yeah, we're Rangers." He pulled down the throttle, gunned the old contraption, and left.

I told friends later of my encounter with the Texas Rangers. "Rangers? Man, you must have looked tough!" It was a year before I saw a Ranger. In the meantime, I wondered. I inquired. Two of them? Later I met a border patrolman. I knew then that I had been accosted that first time by a pair of lowly patrolmen who had taken me first for an alien, then for a sucker—which I was.

My first impression of border patrolmen was "insecure liars," and it has flavored my opinion ever since.

The border patrol had, it is true, a necessary and a thankless job to do. They found us unhelpful in the Valley. We were busy country men. We didn't want to be dictated to. The patrolmen were nosy; they made mistakes; they were never welcome. Most were inexperienced with country problems, so had neither understanding nor sympathy for the farmers.

I don't know the origin of the term, but they were always called "la chota."

Perro

THERE WAS EXCITEMENT ONE HOT, early July morning down the road at the tenant house. Several cars and a paddy wagon were parked there. It looked like my cotton picking crew was being raided. I sent Rikki down in the

pickup to investigate. "No cotton picking today," he came back
and reported. "La chota got them all!"

Later I went down. Raul and Clementina came out of the
house; they had papers of permit to work there, so had not
been picked up. Raul, followed by Perro, his worthless black
dog, walked out to meet me. He was grinning with news and
still nervous with excitement. Freckled Clementina stayed
calmly on the porch holding little long-haired José in her arms.

"La chota, it caught all?" I asked, looking around for sur-
vivors.

"No," Raul laughed. "All, no."

The house was bounded in front by the road and on one
side by the jara-choked barrow pit of an irrigation canal. In
the rear were a couple of abandoned chicken houses and,
farther out in the field, angling rows of extra-tall cotton.

"There remain a few," Raul continued. "They have fear
that la chota will come again and fish them up too."

"How many patrolmen were there?" I asked him.

"Three, Carlos. One in each car and one in the truquecito."

"Three! Why so many?"

"I think that they have been watching for several days,
planning," replied my mustachioed tractor driver, "and decided to swoop down and gather the whole flock this morning.
We saw an airplane circling day before yesterday."

"Did they have time to eat, the people?"

"Some yes, some no."

"Who got away?"

"Hector did. There's his hat still out there," he pointed to
an extra-wide straw sombrero floating atop the tall cotton
plants. "Reimundo stayed. Pedro is down the canal somewhere.
Lorenzo jumped the canal—he flew over."

"In a hurry." I laughed, with a vision of bowlegged Lorenzo
flying.

"Yes," roaring with hilarity, "and Rafael was sitting in the toilet! He watched through a crack."

"Where is he now?"

"He went to town. He fears they will come again."

Square-headed Reimundo heard us talking and came out of the weeds across the road.

"Why, Reimundo! Are you still here?"

"Sí, Carlos. I was washing myself at the cistern without my shirt. I asked la chota for permission to go to my room," he nodded toward the chicken house, "and bring my shirt. He told me to get it. Me, I sat down in a corner on the floor and I forgot to come out. They left me," he grinned wide, "but now I'm afraid they will come again." He went back to his weeds.

A smiling white-shirted man stuck his head above the cotton rows some distance out in the field.

"What are you doing out there, Hector?" I called.

"I crawled between the rows to here," he pointed to his wide sombrero riding the tops of the cotton plants in the gentle breeze. "I dove into the cotton, but my hat didn't want to come. It stayed on top. My hat is over there for la chota to look at—I'm over here. They went, la chota?"

"Yes, but who knows, they might return," I answered. He sank back out of sight.

"Perro, he tore the pants on one man," Raul informed me.

"Perro!" I ejaculated. "You're playing with me, Raul. Perro wouldn't do that!"

"But he did, sí. One policía ran around the house this way, the other ran that way and Perro caught him in the leg and tore his pants. La chota showed me the blood."

"Perro? What a thing muy curioso!"

Perro was a stray of no distinction whatever. He had never even been dignified with a name, only "perro," Spanish for "dog." Of the hands around the place, he had adopted Raul as his patrón, maybe because Raul threw out the scraps. He never barked, never ran, but merely slouched around or slept under the shrubbery. He was not friendly, just neutral. He wasn't suspicious of strangers. He was unnoticeable and un-noticing. He was not even worth getting rid of.

The border patrol raided the house again that night and picked up Alberto and Santos. That made seventeen they had caught from me in one day, a good haul. In a couple of weeks all of the hands were back picking cotton.

Perro was the hero of the crew. They fed him, babied him, talked to him, bragged on him. He ignored them. He ate only when and what he wanted and lay thinking in the shade the rest of the time. But he had had his day. He had sensed danger from enemies of his people, and he had defended them.

A Raid

A CONVOY OF PATROLMEN HIT ARTHUR'S place early in the morning. The hands were preparing for the day: getting breakfast, washing up, and eating. The driveway to the house was short and didn't allow much advance notice of arrivals. But living in daily dread of a sudden raid, the men were always prepared to run, like any creature whose life de-pends on alertness. When the shout "La chota!" came, they scattered like a bunch of chickens being buzzed by a hawk.

Arthur's wife had a little, long-haired dog of an aristocratic breed, I forget what. He was not much of a watchdog; he was everybody's friend and a house dog to boot. But this morning he was ranging in the yard, smelling for news and messages.

When the men ran with such alacrity, the excitement trans-mitted itself to the dog. He grabbed the leg of the nearest patrolman, who happened to be in charge of the raid. He drew blood and tore the pressed pants. The patrolman cursed and drew his revolver.

"Don't you shoot, mister," Arthur called from the back stoop.

"He bit me!"

"I saw that. I'm sorry, but you weren't invited here. You're an enemy of all these men; the dog sensed that. That's what he's for. You shoot him and you'll be in more trouble than you were ever in before."

The irate captain called his men; they took what catch they had, and left. The next day the captain was back with a pronounced limp, his leg bandaged—faking, Arthur thought.

"The health officer in town said you'd better tie up your dog for fifteen days to see if he's got rabies," he told Arthur officiously.

"That," said Arthur, "will not be hard to do. I'll do it."

Three days after the fifteen were over, la chota made another raid. The dog was running loose again.

"I'm not going to get out of the car—you chase them," the captain told his men. "I got bit the last time." The game of hide and seek was soon in full swing. Two wetbacks, flushed out of hiding, streaked past the car for another hiding place. The captain was in a strategic position. He forgot his resolution and jumped out of the car to grab them. As his foot hit the ground, the aristocratic dog fastened onto it. He'd come under the car.

"He drew blood again," the captain raged at Arthur as the convoy left the yard with its captives. "You'll have to tie him up for another fifteen days. I'll be back!"

"We'll be waiting for you," Arthur replied.

He never did come back.

Rural Drama

I TALKED WITH HENRY CANTU, A COT-
ton picking contractor, at the gin. I had a forty-acre tract of
cotton, white with flagging locks. He had a four-bale picking
crew—a crew that could pick four bales a day. "I can handle
all," he said, "no is necessary more people."

"Okay, if you're sure that your people alone can gather it
all."

"Surely yes. You be there in the morning, early, to show me
where to turn in to the field."

So the next morning I was waiting at the corner before daylight. I expected the truck or trucks to come from the east.
The sun was just appearing through the tree tops in town when
from the west I heard a faint engine-roaring. It got louder fast.
It sounded like a big plane, or a sprayer flying low—but this
late in the season? Then I saw the truck barreling down the
road from the west, swaying ahead of its dust, its unmuffled
roar beating the air far ahead.

I was standing in the center of the road that crossed to the
north. Cantu was at the wheel of the truck, very busy driving. I
motioned him on past to the turn. Trailing him closely in
the dust, sometimes neck and neck, was a black car.

Careening wildly to the right in order to make the left-hand
turn, Cantu braked hard. The brakes howled. The following
car, unprepared, went lengthwise into the ditch on the right
and stopped with a thud. The truck made the turn into the
field, but, top-heavy with standing people, it turned over and
skidded on its side. The engine stopped, and screams and
shrieks took the place of its roar.

I was stunned. I collected my wits enough to run around
the end of the canal, into the field, to see better. A wild,
scrambled pile of people writhed on the ground. They were

covered with loose cotton (there had been some in the bed of the truck) and picking sacks, and legs waved like an injured centipede. All over the mass of agitated, loose cotton—in eyes, hair, and clothes—was food from the lunches; frijoles, corn, tortillas, spaghetti, coffee, drinking water. The screeching and wailing went on. I couldn't decide where to take hold first or how to help—but the resourceful country people were already beginning to untangle themselves.

La chota were circling their haul, all three wondering how to take charge. They were only nominally in control. Only Cantu really knew what to do. He simply opened his cab door, now on top, pulled himself up and out, and started shouting at his people to scatter into the cotton field.

One of the bewildered patrolmen careened into me. He looked up wildly and saw a white man, stopped, turned, and looked again.

"Some sonofabitch was standing over there in the center of the road," he panted. "Was that you?"

"I was standing over there," I pointed at the spot, "to show the driver of the truck where to turn in. I don't know about being a sonofabitch. Why?"

"Man, you're lucky! I almost killed you. It was either hit you or go into the ditch. The sun was in my eyes." He was waving his arms as if he were going to take off.

"I didn't know what it was all about." I said. "I was just standing there so the truck driver could see me. —Man, calm down!"

"Well, you—" waving only one arm this time, "well, you're alive." He turned to the pile of human beings to collect what he could.

The pile was coming apart of itself. Kids disentangled themselves first, removing beans and spaghetti from their eyes and mouths. Screaming mothers pulled their youngest out. One man was pulling his woman by her armpits, while she was determinedly hanging on to her baby of six months, who was not yet crying. Men helped their women up, pulling skirts down over knees. Youths strutted, and giggling girls helped with the small children. Cantu was urging them all to scatter, and the patrolmen were circling, giving unheeded orders. They knew they had to take someone into custody, but who? And how? With their car in the ditch, they were afoot.

A highway patrolman showed up with his pad open to write out a citation. How he knew there was trouble out on that country road, I don't know. He conferred with the border patrol, then booked Cantu for failure of brake light.

The pickers were now on their feet and scattered, unhurt. The border patrolmen surveyed the scene and consulted each other hurriedly—you can't shoo a flock of blackbirds into a nonexistent sack. They picked up two men who looked as if they'd been scratched and were standing around. The highway patrolman loaded the border patrolmen and the two wetbacks into his car and left for the hospital, after they had all finished making out their reports—the main concern of all four officers.

Later in the day, Cantu returned with friends and another truck. They righted the overturned truck, undamaged except for the broken taillight—and I think that was an old break.

Directed by the two "injured" men, la chota went out to the wetback camp that night and picked up the rest. The border patrol had seen the truck on the road that morning and had given chase, but Cantu had outfoxed them, keeping them behind in the dust and refusing to let them pass. La chota had gotten madder and madder. They had chased him for three miles, around two other corners, at terrific speeds—sometimes abreast.

Cantu paid a fifteen-dollar fine for traffic violation, I reimbursed him, and so it ended.

That Dumb Mexican

JUAN HAD BEEN WORKING AT ARCHIE'S
for two months. He had quite a wad of one-dollar bills, in spite
of sending most of his money to his wife. He needed some new
work clothes, so Archie took him to a store on East Harriman
where he knew Juan could buy more cheaply the kind of
clothes he wanted.

As Juan and Archie stepped out of the store, they ran right
into a border patrolman sauntering along the sidewalk. He
was in uniform, so he was on duty. There was no way to dodge
him. He knew by looking at him that Juan was wet, and
besides he knew that any Mexican stringing along with Archie
in town was bound to be wet. He knew Archie only by sight
and reputation, so he didn't hesitate to grab Juan while he
had him at arm's length.

Juan was submissive; he had believed all along that the
first time he went to town he would be caught. Archie was
flustered. His usual sang-froid deserted him temporarily. He
was mad at himself for being caught flat-footed, in town of all
places.

"I've got a whole bunch of them out there," he snapped
testily. "Why don't you come out and get them all?"

The patrolman did a double-take and sputtered a bit. This
was not the Archie he'd heard about. He could see that Archie
didn't like him, but an invitation like that could not be
ignored, not in the line of duty. He didn't know where Archie
lived or where his wetback camp was, but he didn't see any
loopholes in the offer.

"I'll just do that!"

"Well," said Archie, "you don't know where they are, so
I'll go ahead. You follow me. You can keep Juan with you."

They went *caminando* out of town and up Highway 281, not too fast, Juan riding with the patrolman. Just before they came to the railroad track an engine whistled for the crossing. Archie, always on the daredevil side, scooted across. La chota might not know many things, but he did know the rules: Public conveyances must stop at crossings. He knew he was safe from being chewed out as long as he followed the rules, so he stopped to let the switch engine and cars pass.

So Archie got ahead. When the train had passed, Juan could still see his white pickup in the distance. The patrolman was not paying close attention, though, so when they came to an intersection Juan pointed west.

"Here is the corner." They turned west, the patrolman trying to catch up with Archie, who was out of sight. At my place, Juan pointed north. At the next corner they turned west again. Then Juan began to seem a little nervous, looking around as if trying to orient himself.

"I don't believe you know where we're going," ventured the patrolman.

"Sí, señor, I do know, very well, where we are going, but I have never been to town before."

"I believe you're lost," asserted la chota a little later.

"No, I'm not. Juan Ortíz never walks lost. Right up here at that corner, you turn to the north again, and that will lead us right to the house of el patrón."

"You're lost," the patrolman announced, with vigor, after the next turn, and following the one after, he was yelling. "You're lost, you damned blockhead!"

"I know where Juan Ortíz lives," Juan insisted. "You go up this road una legua, and we will be at the hacienda of el patrón." He added with dignity, as they finally drove into Archie's driveway, "Juan Ortíz knows where Juan Ortíz lives." Archie's pickup was standing in the driveway, well cooled down. Archie emerged from the house.

"Where in the world have you been?" he called. "I got here a long time ago."

"I don't know where we've been, but I do know that this is the dumbest damned Mexican I ever saw," retorted the fuming patrolman.

"Well, it was his first trip to town. Walked you lost, Juan?"

"No, patrón. We took the wrong turn back there after we crossed the railroad. Don't be mad at me, patrón. I'll never do a thing so stupid again, Don Archie. Por favor, despensame this time, Don Archie." It struck Archie that this excessive politeness was out of character for Juanito—but he caught a twinkle in the man's eye. Poker-faced, he watched for a cue. (From what I heard later from other Mexicans, Juan and la chota must have been gallivanting around a hundred miles or so west of Archie's. Juan took that patrolman for an interesting buggy ride.)

"I'm sorry," Archie explained to the patrolman, "but when I came home none of the men were around here." For Juan's benefit he added, "Se fueron todos." Juan's face registered relief.

"Well, I guess I'll take this man with me then—but he's the dumbest one Mexican I ever saw. He took me on a wild-goose chase all over." La chota waved his arm to the west.

"Yes, he is kind of dumb. I was figuring to get rid of him anyway," Archie agreed. To Juan he said, "It seems to me that you must go with la chota alone. You have been paid."

"Sí, patrón," Juan answered, looking thoughtful. "To me it so seems, and muchas gracias. But, por favor, tell la chota that I would like to get my clothes before I leave. No son muchas."

"He wants to get his clothes before you leave," Archie translated.

"Where are they?"

"Over there in the bunkhouse," answered Archie, pointing to one of the houses in the back.

"Well, tell the idiot to get his clothes and be damned quick about it."

Juan ambled uncertainly toward one of the bunkhouses and went in, leaving the door open behind him. They waited, Archie a little nervous, the patrolman getting madder as the time lengthened.

"What happened to that damned wetback?"

"Juan!" Archie yelled, "hurry up. La chota walks more mad." There was no answer from the bunkhouse. Then Archie thought, That's the only house of the bunch that has a back door!

"Juan!" he yelled again. "You are delaying la chota. Get yourself out here. Prontito!"

La chota got out of his car, fingering his gun, and scrambled crab-like toward the bunkhouse, fast and not in a direct line with the door. He peered in cautiously, then straightened up for a good look and turned to Archie.

"That sonofabitch is gone. He went out the other door."

"I'll be damned," said Archie. "Well, he's out in that cotton field somewhere, then."

The patrolman went to his car, got in, and sat for a while. Archie was silent too. Then the patrolman started his engine and looked at Archie.

"That's the dumbest damned Mexican I ever saw," he said, eased his car into gear, and left.

Coffee Ten Cents

I FIRST HEARD OF MR. GORDON WHEN people began to mention the new coffee shop on the highway just south of town: "I'll meet you at Gordon's," or, "I'll leave it at Gordon's." He soon prospered; after a few years in business he added to his shop, bricked it up, and furnished a room so that small groups could hold meetings and eat at the same time.

Many people went to Gordon's in the mornings—to meet a friend and make arrangements for the day; to have breakfast, if they were early risers and didn't wait for their families to get up; to pick up hands who had promised to be there, or just to pick up available workers hanging around. Men looking for work for the day congregated outside on the bench, or in cold weather went inside to wait and have a cup of hot coffee. Gordon kept lunches already fixed and sacked for laborers, especially wetbacks, who had no one to fix their midday lunches. Coffee cost five cents. It was a busy place, outside and in, at mealtimes, especially early in the morning.

Prices were gradually rising during World War II, and the price of coffee in the cup came in for its share of discussion. Gordon refused to raise his price. He held the line at five cents a cup far longer than anyplace else in town; he made and sold more coffee than anyone else.

His business grew until the border patrol began to realize that Gordon's was a fine place to pick up a load of wetbacks. It was a trap for wetbacks, baited with cheap, hot coffee. Sometimes the patrolmen would wait outside in their car and arrest someone going in. Sometimes they'd go inside and take any wetbacks who happened to be there; if none was there, they might just sit at the counter and wait for some to come in.

It wasn't long before the wetbacks learned that Gordon's was a good place to stay away from, even if the coffee was cheap. Gordon saw that the regular raiding of his coffee shop by la chota was cutting into his business pretty deeply. He fumed and worried, but he couldn't find a solution.

One day I went in looking for someone, and had a cup of

coffee while I waited. A new sign printed in big red letters hung on the wall directly across from the entrance.

COFFEE 5¢ ——— PATROLMEN 10¢

I laughed. "Mr. Gordon, does that sign do any good?"

"You bet it does." He was busy and cut it short. "What do you think I hung it for?"

World Traveler

JUAN BARRERA SHOWED UP ONE MORNING at Vern Talbot's and Vern put him to work. Juan was a loner. He didn't care too much about other people, but lived and cooked alone. His mind just didn't run in the ordinary wet-back slot.

La chota came through one day and cleaned out all of Vern's hands. They came drifting back late; it took a week for the first one to get back. They were disgruntled. La chota had thrown them a fast one. Instead of taking them straight to the bridge, they had taken them to Brownsville, loaded them on a coastal boat, and sent them all the way to Tampico—a town on the Gulf coast a few hundred miles south. They had gotten back to the Rio Grande the best way they could, and some were low on funds. "Qué bárbaro! No?" "Cabrones!"

Juan was the last to get back. It took him two weeks. He was happy and full of bounce: He'd had fun.

"They carried us to Brownsville," he told Vern enthusiastically. "They marched us onto a barco, a big boat, grandote, pure iron. They gave us supper on tables of long boards. The water was very deep, very salty and ugly. We slept on the floor. Plenty of room, plenty of wind, no mosquitoes, no was hot."

"Very good, señor Bern, very, very good. We went all the way to Tampico. So far that we saw nothing of the land! They told us that if we went back to the Estados Unidos, they'd carry us to Tampico another time, or maybe to Veracruz!"

Juan talked Vern's ear off about that wonderful sea voyage. The rest of the men weren't interested in the story, and didn't want to tell anyone else about their own experience. They were ashamed. They felt that they'd been handled like cattle.

A month later, la chota raided a neighbor's field and captured most of his wetbacks. Juan crossed the fence and went over to watch. He laughed and cheered, and got picked up himself. In two weeks he was back—eager to tell Vern about this trip too.

"Muy bueno, Bern. Another ocean voyage! Qué bueno! They feed us very good."

The next time he wanted to go, he simply walked out on the highway and hailed a passing border patrol paddy wagon. They were glad to have him. Later, he flagged them again.

"If you go again on a sea voyage," Vern told Juan after the fifth trip, "don't come back. You can't work for me. No more. Do you understand, Juan? No more."

"Yes—surely. If Juan goes on another ocean voyage, el patrón Bern never will employ him again."

"Exactamente. No come you here again."

But he did. Vern turned him firmly away when he came back. He never saw Juan again, but now and then he heard about him through the grapevine.

"I think he took more ocean voyages," Vern said, "afterwards."

"He really enjoyed his world traveling, eh?"

"Yes. He tried to get in on the airplane rides later, when the patrol first got the planes. I never heard whether or not he got to take one."

Broomcorn

BROOMCORN GROWS IN SLENDER STALKS
from six to ten feet tall. A man of average height can't reach
to cut off the head (brush), so the stalks are broken over. Two
rows are broken over at a time, toward each other so that their
tops intermesh. The finished (tabled) field looks flat from
above—like a giant yellow table about four and a half feet
above the ground. The underside is a giant half-shade, equally
even. The worker can walk in the open between two of these
rows and cut the heads off until he has a handful, then lay
them on top of the table to dry in the sun.

Blufe's men had tabled a field the day before and were
harvesting the heads with short sharp knives when the border
patrol hit with three cars and some paddy wagons. The men
promptly disappeared, ducking into the shade of the tabled
field and slipping away from where they had been. The border
patrol grabbed four men right at the outset who hadn't had
time to get away, locked them in a wagon, and then began to
search in and out of the broomcorn field and the adjoining
orchards.

The hidden men were quiet. They could hear la chota
thrashing around in the cornstalks. When a patrolman got too
close they'd slide over a few rows, staying out of sight. They
were listening intently, but made not a whisper of sound themselves—like quail flowing in the grass. Once in a while a black
head surfaced above the table like a mud hen easing its head
above the still water of a pond, took a quick look, then pulled
back in.

The game went on for three hours with the patrolmen,
sweating in the sun, circling the outside of the field. Finally
they left with only the four men they had caught at first. At
dusk, the men came merrily out of hiding.

"What shall we do?" they asked.

"There's a good moon tonight," said Blufe. "It is best that you keep on cutting tonight. It is sure that la chota will be back tomorrow with more men." The night was cool, with a little breeze. The men finished the field before daylight and left.

At about 7:30 la chota came, with plenty of cars and men. Two airplanes in radio contact with the men on the ground circled the field and the surrounding country. They searched most of the morning. At noon, they left empty-handed.

La Chota Has a Baby

JOSÉ AND LUPE HAD BEEN LIVING IN A tenant house in Bruce's back yard for a year. José was Bruce's irrigator. They had no children, so Lupe worked out, too, when someone needed her.

A young couple, Cleo and Alice Harrow, lived in a house on the adjoining farm. Cleo Harrow was a new border patrolman, and ambitious.

Alice was expecting a baby, so when Lupe stopped there one day and asked for work, Alice, greatly relieved, hired her. Lupe helped her for the month before the baby was due, and took care of the house while Alice was hospitalized. She was there to help when they brought the baby home.

The patrolman had seen José working in the grove before but had never accosted him. The second day the baby was at home, Mr. Harrow didn't want to be away too much—but he wanted something to put on his record for the day. So he questioned José, who was irrigating in the grove, found that he was wet, and took him to the compound in McAllen. It was no skin off the patrolman's nose if the water was left running, unattended. José couldn't argue with him; he didn't volunteer that he had a wife, or tell him who his patrón was, either.

When Bruce came home that evening, he checked the grove. José wasn't there. The water had broken into a neighbor's tomato field, flooding it and ruining the tomatoes. The washout in the border looked as if it had flowed all day.

Bruce hurried back through the orchard to question Lupe.

"I don't know, patrón," she told him anxiously. "I no have seen José since came out the sun. I am much afraid that la chota has carried him off."

Bruce raced over to the McAllen compound. Yes, José was there.

"Why didn't you let me know you had him so we could do something with that water?" Bruce asked Cleo Harrow savagely. "You could have at least done that?"

"That's your problem. I'm not supposed to run around looking for employers. They just give us trouble. My orders are to pick up wetbacks wherever I find them," the patrolman snapped back.

"Well, you're in trouble now," said Bruce. "Let me take José back to take care of that water now. You can pick him up later. Mr. Stanley is going to sue me for flooding his tomatoes."

"It's not my job to look you employers up!" patrolman Harrow repeated with equal heat. "I'm just to pick up the men and see they go back to Mexico."

"But you could bring him back to take care of that water now," Bruce said softly.

"No, I can't. His papers are in the mill now. He's got to go."

"The hell he does!"

"He sure as hell does!"

"Why didn't you pick up his wife, too?"

"His wife? I didn't know he had a wife. He didn't tell me he had one. Where is she? I'll go get her now."

"She's helping your wife with your baby."

There was a short silence. The young man looked stunned.

"Lupe?—Is Lupe his wife? Well, I'll—I'll go get her."

"No, you won't, you bastard. Think! As soon as you go, I'll report you to your chief. You've been using and paying that woman for almost two months. It will explode right under you. You'll be canned, and you'll never get back on the force. And how far will you get finding another job with this on your record?"

Patrolman Harrow was thinking fast.

"Look," Bruce finished, "I've got to get back out there real fast and take care of that water." He left.

Bruce got the water under control and was just getting his wind back when a car drove up in the dusk. José climbed out, suppressing a grin.

"Here's your man," called the patrolman. "Good luck."

"What are we going to do about that tomato field?" Bruce asked.

"I can't help you there. You'll have to figure that out yourself." The engine turned over.

"Okay. Do you want Lupe tomorrow?"

"Yes—we'd appreciate it. Alice is in no shape to be alone."

Lupe worked for the border patrolman's family all that year, until he was transferred. Mr. Harrow never bothered José again, nor did he tip off a fellow patrolman who took his place. José and Lupe were good workers—and Mr. Harrow became a good border patrolman.

One Border Patrolman

"LA CHOTA!" EXCLAIMED A WOMAN softly, drawing in her breath. A black car with a uniformed driver had slipped around the corner unobserved and was upon us. Everyone froze.

Rikki had hitched the H tractor to the machinery trailer and had just driven onto the road from the barnyard. The tractor was idling; the cotton pickers were seating themselves on the trailer. Kelly, with two cotton trailers in tandem behind the C tractor, was still in the barnyard. Some of the wetbacks had been climbing into his trailers, but they scattered into the orchard. The boys had been getting ready to take the crew up to the north forty to pick.

We were caught flat on our bottoms, loaded, all ready for delivery to the wetback stockade down on the Old Depot Road. It was my first time to be caught so completely prepared to turn over my wetbacks.

The car came to a stop in front of Rikki's tractor. The patrolman looked the crowd over, thirty-nine pairs of eyes, including mine, looking back.

"Good morning, Mr. Norquest," he greeted casually.

"Good morning, sir," I said, walking over to shake hands.

"I don't believe you need all these people, do you?"

"Yes, sir, I believe I do. There's forty acres of cotton up there, and thirty-five bales open. I have no way to pick it without them."

"Couldn't you get along with half of them?"

"No, Mr. Horn, I need them all."

Mr. Horn looked the group over. "Mr. Norquest," he puffed on his pipe a few times, "I'm going to quit. I've got a year and a half until I retire. Then I'm going to leave the Valley." The pickers were watching and listening quietly. Very few knew any English. "I'm going to leave this valley so far behind that I'll never see it again."

"Where are you going, Mr. Horn?"

"I'm going to Indiana. I bought a farm up there a few years ago. I'm going to farm that land and fish in my river."

"It's a good life if you can take it," I ventured cautiously.

"Oh, I can take it."

"Did you ever farm, Mr. Horn?"

"No, but I can learn." He kept looking at the people on the trailer. Then he seemed to make up his mind.

"Well, Mr. Norquest, I guess you need them. I'm going down west here," he said, and he eased out his clutch and moved.

Friendly Back Roads

HARRY BORDEN'S COTTON PICKING WAS not going well. He had fifty wetbacks, but even they were not enough. His big field was getting ripe. Any delay from rain or storm, or just weathering, might ruin him. He decided to move the whole crew down there and leave the north fields until later.

The truck driver knew better than to take the highway, but Harry forgot to remind him of the danger from the border patrol, and so he took it. The driver's reasoning was good up to a point: The highway was the shortest route, the pavement meant smoother riding for the standing people in the truck, and there were no corners to negotiate with his top-heavy load. He was about to turn into the home field when a patrol car honked him down.

"Aren't those people wetbacks?"

"That only knows God."

La chota went around the truck asking the people if they were citizens.

"Surely yes," they answered in Spanish. "Somos Americanos."

"Let's see your papers."

"I forgot mine at the house," said one. "Mine are lost," said another. "I don't need papers," said two.

"I think they're all wet," he told the driver. "You turn around and follow me." They went to the compound in McAllen.

Harry was in a tight spot. To lose his pickers at this time was a disaster. He thought of friends in office who might have influence: the sheriff, county judge, district judge, a congressman. He went to each. "That's out of my authority," each told him. "You're outside the law! The border patrol are federal employees and they've got their orders."

Finally late that night he went, hat in hand, to the area captain of the border patrol, with whom he had a speaking acquaintance. Mr. Horn answered his knock at last, coming downstairs in his underwear. He'd been in bed. He was patient, understanding, and, for a man just aroused from sleep, good humored. He listened to Harry's lament.

"I've got to have these people! I've got no other way to gather my crop. I owe the bank, the oil company, the gin, my taxes. I've got a land note to meet. I'm broke, if you won't let my people pick."

"How long will it take, Mr. Borden?"

"To the first of September."

"Mr. Borden, I'm going to let those people pick until Saturday. The rest of this week. But I want you to bring them back Saturday for sure. Do you understand?" Harry was immensely relieved. They both knew the pickers would filter back to the work before the weekend was through.

"But, Mr. Borden," the captain added, "don't come parading down the highway with that crew on display like you did today. We can't just ignore them. Can't you find some dirt roads?"

Frozen Fish

IT WAS AFTER MIDNIGHT ON THE THIRD night of a norther. The wind had stopped. It was bitter cold, and the sun would bring a heavy frost.

I was out on wetback business in the pickup. When the cab became unbearably cold, I went to a restaurant in North Mission for some hot coffee. I drank slowly and began to warm up a little. I was about to leave when the door opened and a border patrolman, a kind of elderly man, came part way through and shouted to the waiter.

"Pete—I've got a pair of frozen bastards out here. Have you got something hot back there to feed them?"

"Only the usual breakfast, Cap'n, but I can heat up some canned chile."

"Do that. Two of them. Give them some coffee now. They're going to conk out on us if we don't get something hot into them. They're soaked." He turned back and shouted to his partner in the car, "Bring them in, Ben!"

The patrolmen came in guiding two miserable Mexicans. Their clothers were sodden and they had no hats. One had lost his huaraches. Their collarless shirts were thin. They were like fish brought out of the water from under the ice—only half aware. The patrolmen pushed them toward the back to the kitchen door, where it was warmer, sat them down, and slid cups of coffee to them. They were bewildered but not frightened.

The captain said, "Drink you the coffee. Warm up the gut. You have yet plenty voyage. You are going through Hidalgo. It's going to freeze when comes out the sun. Andale!" They drank the coffee, got refills, and began to work on chile and crackers. They brightened up some and answered a few questions. They wanted to pick fruit.

"Well, but you're not going to gather the fruit, like this.

You're going back home again. Understand? Over there on the other side," the captain said. He turned toward me and lowered his voice. "We ought to have a place to put them over here—feed them a little when we catch them." He and the younger patrolman sat down at a table, and Pete brought them coffee.

"Where did you pick them up, so fresh from the water?" I asked them.

"On a cross trail in that jungle below Granjeno. They acted like they wanted to be caught. I guess they were too cold. We thought we could find an eating place open over in South Mission to warm up the poor soaked bastards, but we had to bring them clear up here."

I eased casually up to the Mexicans. "Why are you so wet on a night like this?"

"Well," one looked at the other, "the lancha turned itself over. We were very near the American side. I think it was Pepe who upset it. La culpa is his."

"Yes," answered Pepe slowly, "the fault is mine. It hurt, my leg, it cramped. La lancha was too small. I tried to ease my leg; I was sitting on it."

"He died, anyone?" I asked.

"No. Pepe and me, we climbed out, on the side of the Estados Unidos. The water was deep."

"And the lanchero, what happened to him?"

"He followed la lancha in the current and took it to the bank. He's a turtle, him."

"He returned to the other side?"

"Sí, señor."

The men had dried out some. The captain was in a hurry to get them on the walkway of the bridge, headed for Mexico. They finished their big bowls of chile; then la chota hurried them out into the quiet cold.

"I never saw la chota feed them before," I remarked to Pete.

"Oh, yes. Old Cap'n, he comes in here every once in a while, if the place is empty, with some hungry mojados that he's caught just after they crossed. Generally they haven't eaten for a long time—went broke getting to the border."

"Well, it's unusual."

"Yes. Old Cap is okay. He don't stand for any monkey business—he'll cut them down to size, all right, if he needs to. But he's fed a lot of those poor devils before he sent them back; out of his own pocket, too."

Legalized

WHEN THE BRACERO PROGRAM CAME into effect, we heard that, if we wanted men, we had to take them as they came. We didn't want just anyone; we wanted our own men, the men we knew and had trained, who knew us, our farms, our working habits. It almost created an impasse, but the officials finally found a loophole in the law, so that we could get the men we wanted.

I got my men the first time around, processing and insuring them successfully. They all passed their physicals, except Andrés.

"Come on, people." I urged, "get in the pickup. Vamonos! Let's go."

The fifteen men exchanged glances and shuffled their feet.

"No, Carlos," they said, "we want to spend a little time in Reynosa before we come. You wait a little time here on the United States side. In a little while, too, we will come. We want to celebrate a little. You wait."

They went trailing single-file back across the bridge. I think they wanted the out-of-this-world satisfaction of coming back across it, into the United States—legally. For upon getting their papers in their hands, they changed in some way: a look in the eye, a straightening of the back, a more mature expression. I felt that they wanted to strut a little up on the square, get a drink or two, show their prized papers to any friend they chanced to meet.

I waited for an hour before the first one came back. He had become separated from the rest, gotten worried, and headed for the bridge and the pickup.

"Where are the other people?" I asked.

"I don't know. I thought they had come to the truck. I hurried."

Later we saw three more on the footpath to the other end of the bridge. They were in no hurry. They sauntered along, looked down over the rail at the water, pointed, stopped, continued slowly.

"Where are the others?" they asked, coming up to us.

"Where did you leave them? They haven't come."

"At the cantina, but they were ready to follow."

"They must have taken another swallow or two," I said.

Then the rest showed at the other end of the footway. They too were sauntering, chesty. They were enjoying themselves, strutting, hats cocked, walking tall. They stopped to talk a little, to peer over the rail at the muddy water below. They were high above and could see far up and down the river. They pointed and laughed.

Of all the times they had gone back and forth, this was the first time they had come across from Mexico on the bridge like men. They had gone back home lots of times over the bridge; no one ever questioned them as they returned to Mexico. But this was the first time in their lives that they had come across that bridge going north to the United States. They had graduated from nothing to something. They were walking as men should walk—upright—glancing to neither the left nor the right in fear.

They walked past the customs, liquor tax collector, immigration. They showed the new papers with their pictures on them and looked all of those uniformed Americans in the eye. They were expansive; not drunk, just feeling good, like a bunch of happy kids.

The transformation was worth going fifteen miles to see.

CHAPTER SEVEN

Citizens and Migrants

LIKE EVERYBODY ELSE, OUR LOCAL LA-
boring people liked to take a trip once a year. They readied
their car or truck, making it as self-sufficient as possible, filled
it with friends, picked enough cotton here to pay for the gas,
and headed *al norte*—to the north. They generally made money
on their trips, but weren't too disappointed if they didn't. They
had fun, learned their way around in the north, established
contacts for the next year. Even when this area was a partial
labor vacuum, wide open to wetbacks, most wetbacks who could
find a berth in a vehicle going al norte, went. A few, on the
other hand, stayed here, worked, became citizens and residents,
raised their families here. Their stories are worth telling, too.

The migrants have become more and more sophisticated.
Highways to the north are paved and cars and trucks are more
roadworthy and bigger. Now, many board up their winter
homes here while they're gone, coming back only to put their
kids back in school. The bigger the family, the more profitable
their trips. They come back and replace their homes with bigger
ones, board them up, and leave again. There's one house between here and town that's been boarded up for fifteen years.
The owners come back every few years, clean up the yard, paint
the house, then lock the gates of the hurricane fence around
the yard, and hurry back north.

Shoe Business

FELIPE CAME FROM GUANAJUATO WITH his wife and two children, a little boy and a little girl. He'd saved enough money for their train fare to the border at Reynosa, and had enough left to pay a lanchero to take them across the river. They crossed the Rio Grande one breezy, starlit night, quartering across with the wind and landing on a low spit on the Texas side.

Felipe and Sofia took up a child apiece and started north by the stars. They were hungry and tired. They knew no one on this side of the river. They walked until they were too tired to go any farther, then stopped in a clump of huisaches away from the road and slept. In the morning, they ate what food remained in Felipe's morral and started north again, staying off the roads. They went on until they came to a nursery where citrus trees were being developed for planting. The men working there told them that el patrón might need more help and suggested that they wait for him.

The patrón, Guy Wilson, hired Felipe to help in the nursery. He took the family over to his buildings and gave them a one-room house. Felipe worked for Guy for two years, budding trees.

Felipe was a shoemaker by trade. He did handwork. Guy helped him get a job with the local shoe repair man in Pharr, where Felipe worked steadily for five years, learning to handle electric shoe repair machinery, and to speak English, and how they did business in the United States. He was earning enough money to support his family, but his family was growing. They needed more food and clothes, a bigger house, schooling. He talked with shoe machinery salesmen. He rented a cubbyhole three doors west of his patrón's shop and bought used machinery at the smallest possible capital investment.

Then once he was picked up on the street by a border patrolman. He was back in Pharr the next day.

"How did you get back here?" I asked him.

"I swam."

"You left your family here?"

"Yes, I never told la chota that I had a family here, and I never told them where I worked."

"Did you go to Guanajuato to visit?"

"No. I came straight back, that night the same."

"Then they must have turned you loose in Mexico as you arrived."

"Sí. They turned us loose. I walked east from Reynosa about two miles, then right down to the river and swam back."

He was picked up by the patrol many times after that. He never mentioned his family to the patrol. His family knew, when he didn't come home, that he was on another forced trip to Mexico. One of them would go over to the shop to see that everything was in order and to put up the temporary "Closed" sign. They'd await the return of their breadwinner, and soon Felipe would get back, rested and refreshed.

"My oldest boy," he told me, "went through Pan-American College, spent two years in Vietnam, got married, and worked in a dry goods store in McAllen. A good job. My second boy is now through high school and is going to the war. My oldest girl is married and has two little ones. You should see them. Americanos puros!"

Felipe finally finagled some work papers. He got tired of all those trips to Mexico. The family never became migrants.

He has all kinds of well-oiled machinery in his shop. He has a small stock of boots and other leather goods to sell. All were bought with as small a down payment as possible; he is now paying off his debts in prosperity. His shop isn't as spick-and-span as it might be, but it's comfortable. He has a counter across the room making a show area for his stock, a soft drink machine, a few comfortable chairs, a domino table. It is a lounging area for his friends.

"Are you ever going back to Mexico?" I asked him.

"No. Our children are American. I'm a stranger in Mexico."

"How many do you have now, Felipe?"

"I have ten. My oldest quit his job in McAllen and is getting three seventy-five an hour for Caterpillar work in Fort Worth. All the rest who are big enough to work are ocupado in town."

Life flows leisurely for Felipe. He smiles much. He always has a good car for the family, a good pickup for business. His former employer and present competitor down the street laughs and says, "Yes, Felipe is doing all right. He's fattened the wrinkles out of his belly. The joke is on me. I trained him— made a good craftsman of him. Then when a lot of my customers had befriended him and he had a big following, he pulled up stakes and opened up for business three doors down.

"Oh, I've got plenty of business. There's enough for us both. But I never get over the feeling that somehow the joke is on me."

Serrucho

"SERRUCHO?"

"Sí, Carlos?"

"Were you mojado when you first came over?" He was rushing around with his work. He placed the block under my front axle to check the loose steering linkage.

"Sí, Carlos, I was wet. I swam the river."

"Alone?"

"Yes, solito. I wasn't foolish. I wasn't going to pay twenty-five pesos to some bandido to take me across in a boat."

"You told me that you came from Veracruz. Did you come alone from there?"

"Sí, Carlos. I was fourteen. Like now, I was big and fat."

"That's a long way for a kid."

"Yes, but Carlos, I was leaving Veracruz for always. I intended to stay in the Estados Unidos. I thought to become an American at once."

He wasn't coming over here just to earn some money and go back. He was coming for always. He got off the bus at Reynosa about noon, asked where the river was, and went to find it. He was a little better dressed than most wetbacks, and he went unnoticed. He walked down to the river, looking for a good place to enter and a good place to come out. About dusk, after walking the curving bank for several miles, he found a place he liked.

He'd left the town and its crowds behind. He undressed, tied his clothes in a tight bundle, entered the warm water, and swam across holding the bundle above his head with one hand. He hit the north bank in the mud and climbed out. He dressed as soon as he'd dried in the breeze a little, and climbed up the second bank.

Serrucho was fourteen, he knew no English, he was in a strange country, but his expectations were high. They still are.

He knew where north was, so he walked in that direction through the huisaches and ash. He came to a field road heading in about the same direction and followed it, his heart light. Where the dirt road joined a graded road, a cluster of houses stood. The dogs barked. Serrucho kept going. He wanted to get as far away from the river as he could.

He found a paved crossroad and followed it. He was dressed well and his clothes were dry. No one bothered him, although there were a few cars on the pavement. The road made a big swing to the north and he followed that for several miles. The houses got thicker. Then he was in a town. He passed

through it and was in the country again, following the pavement openly like any local resident. After many miles the road
turned to dirt, and he followed that in turn. Finally, feeling
safer, he turned in at a farmhouse. The owner was American,
but could speak some Spanish. "Yes," he told Serrucho, "I
can give you work around here and in the store." But it rained,
rained, rained. It rained for thirty days. It was too wet to work
outside.

"Mr. Leon fed me. I stayed and worked for him for two
years, in the yard and in the store. I was treated well. I wanted
something else, though, something ahead of me. The railroad
was close. I'd go over and watch the section crew work. I
wanted to work there, so Mr. Bob offered me a job on his
maintenance crew. I was sixteen, but big. I worked for him for
a year. I stayed at a little colonia along the track.

"I walked the railroad into town at first; it was safer. Then
I went on the highway after I got more English. I passed a
garage. I stopped many times to watch the mechanics work.
This was what I wanted to do. The owner offered me twenty
dollars a week to clean parts—wash the grease off the engines
for the mechanics. I walked four miles to work.

"El patrón gave me a new bicycle. It was in a box. He told
me, 'You put that together and I'll give it to you. You work
for me good, and I'll make a mechanic of you.' That was the
very thing I wanted. That was in forty-two. He paid me thirty
dollars a week.

"Four years later he told me, 'Serrucho, you don't need any
more schooling. You work by yourself.' I was on commission;
the more work, the more pay. A few years later, I bought a
1938 coupé for two hundred dollars. I paid el patrón twenty
dollars a month.

"During all of these years I had never been stopped by la
chota. But driving this car in to town one day I found they
had a road block, stopping everybody. 'Are you a citizen?'

'Yes.' 'Let's see your papers.' 'I have none. I'm a citizen but my license is at home.' I could talk pretty good English. They let me pass. That's the only time I was ever stopped. I passed for an American everywhere.

"I worked on a fifty-fifty basis for twelve years. Then el patrón started to fix up papers for me. He gave me ten dollars a week to pay my sustencia to stay in Reynosa for four months and establish residence there. He took me to the courthouse to arrange citizen papers. Mr. Garza and Mr. Smith witnessed.

"In 1950 I married an American girl and lived with her for a year. Then I divorced her. She tried to boss me all the time. Serrucho, do this; Serrucho, do that.

"Two years later, I married again and bought a half-acre on this paved road to build a little house. My wife had chickens, a pig, some goats, but no kids came. 'Why, with all of these animals to take care of, you have no kids?' I asked her.

" 'Well, none come!'

" 'I want some kids!' "

" 'Well, you'll have to go and buy one!'

"We went to the Hidalgo clinic and adopted one. I bought another half-acre of land adjoining. I built a shed and started to work for myself; I opened a garage.

"El patrón got mad. He didn't speak to me for two years. Then one day he called me on the telephone. 'Serrucho, why do you not buy new parts from me?'

" 'Patrón, I thought that you didn't want to sell me parts.'

" 'Sure, Serrucho, come here and buy parts. I'll let you have all you want, at a discount, on credit if you wish.'

"I bought new cars, a service truck, another half-acre. I like this country. The people are nice. We adopted another baby, a girl, from the Hidalgo clinic. I bought another half-acre of land and now have two acres here. All the room I need for my business.

"I worked for the old patrón twenty-one years. I think that's enough. No? I now buy lots of parts from him. I work two men now all the time."

Businessman

CIPRIANO PICKED COTTON FOR ME FOR two years. Fresh from Aguas Calientes, he was young, agile, and athletic, but there was nothing to indicate that he might be out of the ordinary. The next year he and his compadre left me in midseason to pick for a landowner about twenty-five miles to the north who promised them other work after cotton picking was over.

Five years later, Cipriano stopped to visit on his way back to his patrón after a trip to Mexico. It was not cotton picking season. He was grubbing—clearing land up north by contract, for so much an acre.

Elías, the Spanish-speaking landowner, had inherited thousands of acres handed down from an ancient land grant. Under a soil conservation contract with the government, he was clearing it of monte and chaparral. He employed Mexican nationals by the hundreds, at first as wetbacks, later as braceros. He built long barracks and dining halls for them according to government specifications. He could have cleared the ground with bulldozers and other big machinery, but he stuck with his men. He'd need them in the coming years to pick cotton again.

Cipriano was one of these hundreds. He apparently had no close ties in Mexico. He stayed over here all the time, always available for work and adaptable to any kind. He made himself valuable to Elías, who grew to depend on him to keep the patrón's wife's flowers producing and the grass mown. Cipriano was a good fixer, and the patrón lived twenty-five miles from the nearest repair shops.

Elías introduced Cipriano to the banking procedure in this country. Cipriano was an industrious grubber; he earned well and banked his money regularly. The patrón encouraged him to get his citizenship papers.

Cipriano came by my home every few years for a visit. He'd tell me what he was doing, what he was thinking of doing. He seemed to value my opinion—I don't know why.

Later, he moved to town. He wanted a business of his own. He'd labored for fifteen years. Now he wanted something easier, more interesting, more rewarding. He studied the town, rented a little wooden building on a main street, and went into the fruit business. He prospered. He courted and married a local girl with a high school education. He expanded the business to include vegetables. He either was a natural at it or he had some know-how from Mexico, for he did well even though his perishable stock was dynamite to handle and competition was rough.

He bought the property his business stood on. He expanded continually. When he'd been in business ten years he was including a lunch counter. His wife drove a nice car and Cipriano a pickup.

Two lots, one on a corner and the other between the corner lot and his business, came up for tax sale. Cipriano wanted them, and, as his English was not too good, he asked a friend to bid for him.

"How high shall I go?" asked his friend.

"Follow it up to sixteen thousand dollars," said Cipriano.

The lots were sold to him for twelve thousand five hundred. Cipriano stripped the money from a roll and paid there and then.

Santiago

"I'D LIKE TO GET MY HANDS ON THAT Mexican. I'd like to see him just once. We've got a dossier on that sonofabitch that thick!" The immigration officer at Hidalgo held his hands apart three inches. "It goes clear back to World War I!"

"You mean Santiago Sepulveda?"

"Yes, I mean Santiago Sepulveda! A smuggler."

"I can't believe it! He's worked for me off and on for ten years, wet."

"It's the same sonofabitch, all right. And if I ever get hold of him, I'll shut him up so tight he'll never get out." He stopped to light a cigarette. "He's slick as an eel. I've got a dozen sworn statements from him that he's a Mexican citizen, and I've got a dozen sworn statements from him that he's an American citizen!"

Our soft-spoken Santiago. I'd noticed that at times he seemed a little shifty-eyed, but he'd been absolutely square with me. I'd lent him plenty of money at different times. His daughter Carmen had been born in the machine shed on my other place one cold night, during a blue norther; the shed had caught fire from the tub of coals they used to keep warm, and they'd put out the fire, scrambling to bring water from the cistern in buckets. Carmen had prospered.

"Don't bring that bird around here too close or we'll nab him. I've been wanting to set eyes on him for fifteen years," threatened another immigration officer one hot summer morning at the bridge as I was trying to process Santiago and some other men as braceros.

I expect our mild, tobacco-chewing Santiago had crossed that bridge two hundred times since it was built, right past their office door, always on his way back to Mexico. Plenty of times he'd crossed the river on the ferry, too, before the bridge was built. And in the water—well, Santiago swam like an eel, underwater or on top. He lived at Quatro Palmas. He was married to a de León—the oldest sister to the seven brothers.

Santiago talked to me many times about being born at Beeville, Texas. But he had no birth certificate. He claimed that the priest there had not given his father one, and most likely he hadn't. Chances were that Santiago had never been near a church there when he was little. He was illiterate, and I expect his dad was too, and would have attached little importance to a paper even if the family had been given one.

As Santiago grew older, he wanted more and more to be wholly American. His aging limbs cried for it. Somehow, he had brought his big, fat wife over here so the last baby could be born in the United States—in my machine shed. I'd helped him to get the baby registered here.

I went with Santiago several times over the years to Edinburg to talk with a local priest. I wrote several letters to the incumbent priest in Beeville, who always sent back a neatly typed testimonial with whatever information Santiago wanted him to put on it.

But nothing happened, and the immigration officials still said, "I'd like to get hold of that sonofabitch," or "I'd like to set eyes on him, just once!"

I don't know how Santiago finally wangled papers—but he has them. They are precious. He keeps them wrapped in plenty of cellophane in his shirt pocket. Often when he's talking he absent-mindedly pats to see if they're still there. He nows walks safe.

He comes around sometimes with one of his sons to see me. He has gotten papers for some of them, too; lawyer-fixing, I think, for every once in a while I get a telephone call from some lawyer wanting a bit of information, generally a date. One son, Salvador, came into the yard recently with a new pickup—full of his kids, American citizens. Chepo is apparently a dirt-moving tycoon in Mexico, using big machinery; he comes around sometimes in a big car, fat. Fernando has a carload of kids too. Carmen grew into a handsome woman. She married a Mexican national and has eight kids and more in the hopper —all born in Mexico but claiming American citizenship through her.

Santiago is a successful man. He may not have property— but he's alive, he's a United States citizen, he has about a million descendants, and Social Security provides him with plenty of Lobo Negro to chew.

From Wetbacks to Migrants

OVER THE YEARS FROM TWENTY-NINE ON, Jack financed eighteen wetbacks and their dependents to U.S. citizenship. He was going to make it easy, for them and for himself, to have them work here.

The first one, Alfredo Ruís, was the best of the bunch. He worked for Jack for seventeen years. He had a wife and two children. He bought and paid for the house he lived in; he wanted to do it. When he left, he moved the house to a colonia north of Jack's place and stayed here in Hidalgo County. He didn't migrate.

The one who stayed next longest worked for Jack for five years after he got his papers. He drove into the yard one day in a 1920 Ford that he'd bought in Detroit on a work safari to Michigan. He had all ten of his kids with him in that Ford when he arrived that afternoon from Monterrey, Nuevo León. Later when his kids got big enough to work and help with family expenses, he migrated to Michigan. They became migrant workers. They earned plenty of money. He bought new cars to travel in; at one time the family had five. The older kids got married and had families. Their official home base is near Jack's now. Every spring they go north, the whole tribe, a caravan. Jack feels quite patriarchal about them.

Next was a group of five brothers, big men, one of whom was married. They stayed around just until they all had their papers, then left for the north. Six more migrants. They didn't have to serve in either the American army or the Mexican army during the war.

He helped another bunch of single boys, cousins to the first five. One of them worked a week after he got his papers, the others not at all. Two other families stayed with him for a couple of weeks after they got their papers, then left for the north. There were others—all of whom went north when they became citizens.

The last one stayed for a few years. He came to Jack's place with a suitcase full of clothes and a girl.

"Is this your wife?" Jack asked him.

"No, she's a friend."

"If you are going to work for me, you've got to get married," Jack told him.

The neighboring Mexicans built up a big wedding for them. He stayed two years. Jack taught him how to overhaul his tractors. The man was a natural mechanic. He got a job in a tractor agency in town—learned automatic transmission mechanics. He moved to town. It took four pickup loads to move just the property he had accumulated in the two years.

"He'll always have a job," said Jack. "But I think I've helped my last Mexican with his papers. Most of them never even thanked me."

Migrant Factory

CARL WAS A DAIRY MAN AND USED HELP all the time, seven days and nights a week. Ricardo was a wetback who worked for him, a hard worker and always dependable. Ricardo brought his family over and established them in a small house on the property.

Every year or so another baby came, until there were twelve. Every year or so, another room was added to the little house. Ricardo's children went to school on the bus, through the grades and then on to high school. With Carl's guidance, Ricardo changed from wetback to bracero, then to citizen.

He and his wife raised a very nice family, but school spoiled the children for work as Ricardo knew it. He expected some help from them when they got big enough to work, but it didn't materialize. His wife, after years of observing the histories of other families, decided that her children were not going to slave like their father. She was against their going into the fields, but there was no other work they could do besides in agriculture. Instead of helping then, they were always asking for a little spending money.

Ricardo's family had graduated from a walking family to a pickup, then a two-pickup, family. Things tightened up all over for Ricardo. He felt that the children only wanted what they could get from him. His spouse was no longer a wife to him. She even objected to his occasional beer drinking, saying, "This beer drinking is not necessary. It is not so in good families."

Ricardo finally cracked and broke under the strain. He disappeared, and they didn't hear from him. The kids had to go to work, and became migrant workers. Several years passed. Then a migrant laborer reported seeing Ricardo in Nampa, Idaho. The next season Ricardo's family asked a truck-driving migrant who was taking a crew to Washington state to look up Ricardo when he went through Nampa. A year later the truck driver was back.

"He is very fine, Ricardo," he reported. "He is prospering. Has a good job, all the beer he wants, and a woman. He has no shame for running away. 'There was nothing but slavery left for me at home,' he said. He told me, 'Estan bastante grande los muchachos—the kids are plenty big, no? To take care of themselves and their mamá. Some of them are married, no?' Like that he thinks."

Ricardo wanted his freedom. He had done his bit.

Citizen Material

I DON'T REMEMBER WHEN TRICIO FIRST showed up around the farm wanting work. He was middle-aged, illiterate, and not very bright. He could hoe and do stoop work well, but much patience was needed to teach him to irrigate, to handle water intelligently. Anything that needed thought floored him. For that reason I could not use him steadily.

After one trip to Mexico, he brought back his wife Manuela, and two daughters, Carolina (ten) and Sarita (four). I provided them with a little house.

Manuela was a short, stout, energetic person whose talk never ended. Her ready smile was contagious. She kept poor Patricio under her thumb; he adored her for it, and listened attentively. She managed the money and made the decisions, and Tricio said nothing and smiled. Carolina was a vivacious little girl, but not loud like her mother. Little Sarita had a cleft palate. Her speech was garbled and unintelligible. Manuela and Patricio kept her hidden as much as possible. They were ashamed of her, I guess. She was extremely shy.

One day Manuela came and asked for work in the house. Lee needed help. She tried Manuela out at cleaning rooms and found her very efficient. Manuela had her own ideas about how to do things, and strongly preferred her own methods. She wasted no time, and liked to tell about the fine houses in which she had worked in Monterrey, Mexico, where they were from. Then she'd vary the theme with how nice her own house in Monterrey had been; what nice furniture, what nice things. We wondered why they left it all and come across the river. Manuela never tried to explain this. We decided that she was identifying with her employer in her mind.

Then, when our Mark was about to be born and Lee needed her badly, Manuela decided it was time to quit. No persuasion would move her. No, she wasn't dissatisfied; she just wanted to quit. I think her own importance was growing on her; she felt that it was demeaning to work for country folks.

They bought a cheap lot in town and Manuela somehow managed on their wages to build a new one-room house and paint it green. Carolina started to school and learned English. Patricio was then working for Uncle Poppie pretty steadily. Poppie consulted the health authorities about little Sarita. They sent her to San Antonio and had the cleft closed. She came out of hiding, began to talk understandably, and started to school.

We think that Manuela had developed a need to identify, to relate her own importance to that of those around her, and that that was the reason she left us. We were only farm people. She got a job with a lawyer's wife in town, and basked in the reflected importance of the lawyer.

Old Tricio plodded on. He'd learned to handle water and had all the work he could do. Manuela managed, through the lawyer, a beginning toward citizenship. She heard of the wonderful wages in the northern states. She got a trucker, a labor contractor, to take them along.

They made more money there and came home less and less. Carolina married a Polish farmer's son, they said. Sarita developed into an attractive teenager. I haven't seen any of them for many years now. I think they are in Indiana for good.

Manuela was ambitious.

A Credit

WHEN I FIRST KNEW MIGUEL, HE WAS living in a tule shack on a low spot over by the big dirt canal a half-mile east of here. Every time it rained heavily the water covered his earthen floor. The Valley is arid, so this happened maybe once a year. I thought of him as a wetback, and I've never had reason to change my opinion. He'd never been to school. He could sign his name, but only he could read what he had written.

"Miguel, I have known you many years. Tell me, where from are you? Where were you born?" I asked him once. He didn't answer immediately, but stood thinking for a little.

"Carlos, I must be honest. I don't know. God only knows."

"Your parents never told you, Miguel?" He wrinkled his forehead and looked up at me from under his eyebrows.

"I don't know my parents, Carlos. I never knew who they were. I lived with some people."

I never asked him any more. I felt that for some reason Miguel didn't want to talk about it, and I think he had already told me all he knew.

Miguel married Pabla, the second daughter of a proud old Texan, Narsiso, who squatted on a corner of my place in a tule shack. Old Narsiso had five kids. He had never gone to school in his life and thought it unnecessary for his own children to go. In those days the woods were full of families like this. There were no truant officers, no graded country roads—only *breachas*, cleared alleyways where the roads were supposed to go.

What is poverty? Miguel, born to poverty, was a worker, and honest. His family never was hungry, always had passably good clothes—sometimes better than mine. He learned how to bud citrus trees and worked steadily for years and years in a nursery. For those times he made good money. By paying his poll tax regularly, registering for the draft, and performing civic duties, he established his residency beyond question and carried many legal papers to show to anyone who questioned him.

The kids kept arriving until they had a family of about eight. The older ones were ready to do some income work, and Miguel had a work force of his own. He used them in a body, but he kept the children in school. He bought a used truck, loaded the kids in the truck, and took them north to work. He established a regular itinerary through the northern states in the vegetable raising areas from Washington to Ohio, and was gone about half of each year.

Every year or two he brought home another second-hand vehicle. The family came and went in a caravan, extremely mobile, carrying all of life's necessities with them. He sent some of the children home when school resumed each fall.

Later Miguel bought two ten-acre tracts of land, built himself a nice home on one and put small houses on it for his children when they married.

Now Miguel wears glasses and carries a notebook and pencil. He's a businessman, even if he is illiterate; he has his children write in the notebook for him. His kids stayed in school and speak good English. One is a businessman in town. One girl, a beauty, teaches school. One is a border patrol officer. All the rest are substantial citizens, too, although two married Mexican nationals and are retracing their father's footsteps, going Mexican again.

The Mayan

PEDRO BUSTAMENTE, THIN AND ANXIOUS, came to Tom's place one morning in the early fifties looking for work. He had a wife and four children waiting for him in a one-room shack in town. They were hungry. They'd waded the Rio Grande about a week before, the river was very low from the seven-year drouth. He'd found a little work, but he had to pay a dollar a week in rent for the little house; he needed steady work.

Pete was a small man—although big for an Indian—and very dark. Tom thought he might look bigger if fattened up some. He was in his early thirties. His right hand had been crippled by an untreated cow-herding injury.

Tom was a town farmer. He had a business in McAllen, but lived with his family three miles or so northwest on a small tract. He needed someone regular to keep the place going: feeding, milking, repairing, yard work. Pete could milk, so Tom hired him.

Pete's wife was short too; plump, dark, wide in the face. They were Mayans from Yucatán. Pete talked a queer sort of Spanish. He was used to walking, and walked back and forth the three and a half miles from town to work. He kept Tom's

Jersey cow staked out on grass and the two families in milk and cream.

Late one night, when Pete had been irrigating all day and had finished after midnight, Tom drove him home. Two hours later, a McAllen policeman called.

"Tom, we have a man here who says he's yours."

"What's his name?"

"Pedro Bustamente, he says."

"A crippled hand?"

"Yes."

"He's my man, all right. What's he done?"

"He about killed another Mex a while ago. The neighbors called. He caught the man in bed with his wife, and slammed him in the head with a brick. The other guy's bleeding. He's in the hospital."

"Is he going to live?"

"Doc says so."

"What have you got Pete charged with?"

"Nothing yet. He's just sitting here. I don't blame him. I'd have done the same thing; you too."

"Yeah, I guess I'd have killed the man. Well, Fred, what are you going to do with Pete?"

"Charge him with a misdemeanor of some kind, I guess. He's not dangerous. If I let you come and get him, Tom, will you be responsible for him?"

"Sure I will."

Tom signed bond and took Pete back to his family, and Pete came back to work. Two days later he reported that his wife had disappeared with the baby boy. Pete asked if he could come to live on Tom's ranch and have his little girls there with him. Tom had an old hay barn that Pete said they would be happy to have for quarters, so Tom took the little family home with him.

The girls, twelve, nine, and five, cleaned out a section of the barn to camp in. Tom ran electricity out, put in some lights, and found a usable old refrigerator, a hot plate, and a radio. He piped water out to them, put in partitions, and paid Pete's court costs. The injured man recovered, and Pete's wife stayed lost.

Juana, leggy and dark, was in charge under Pete. Next was blonde Raquel (probably a former indiscretion of their Indian mother), who had had some schooling in Mexico in writing and arithmetic. They kept themselves and little Rosa scrubbed and very clean; kept the living quarters clean.

It seemed that Pete was going to devote his life to these three girls. He sent the older two to school on the bus, and kept chubby little Rosa with him all the time. Pete was dense about learning English; it just didn't come for him, but the girls picked it up fast. They played with Tom's kids and always insisted on speaking English with them.

Pete took Tom's children under his wing, too. He taught them Mayan handicrafts, how to splice ropes, throw a lariat, do leather work, repair fences. He had a way all his own with kids, unlike most wetbacks. He understood their need for guidance and attention.

Every Saturday afternoon Tom took the family to town. He arranged credit for them at a store for supplies. They'd buy their supplies, leave them in the store, and go to a movie. A store employee would bring them home in the evening in time to do chores.

In the late fifties, the border patrol became more determined. On orders from above, it recruited many new patrolmen to clear the Valley of wetbacks. Tom and Pete began to worry. They decided they had better get the family legalized as quickly as possible. Pete had too many counts against him to do it fast; he was separated from his wife, he had a police record in town, he was living in the United States, he spoke no English.

Pete got a quickie divorce in Tamaulipas. He obtained a letter of good repute from the county sheriff's record (by-passing the city police). He moved to Reynosa for two months to establish Mexican residency. The priest there got their birth certificates from the Yucatán churches. It took time and money. Tom paid all the expenses, including plenty of *mordida* (bill-padding) on all the Mexican items. At last the excited, happy family got its papers.

Pete got itchy feet. He wanted to go north, as almost all wetbacks did when they became naturalized citizens. He talked it over with Tom. He wanted to give his girls a good education and make Americans of them—to raise them with only gringos around them.

He moved north to Washington state—but with this difference from so many other wetbacks: He stayed. He didn't become a lifetime migrant, following the climate and spending his money traveling. The girls all went through high school there. Juana married, and Raquel was spoken for.

Then one December day there they all were in Tom's yard, well dressed, driving a good car. They had driven clear across the United States just for a two-day visit with the Wilsons.

"Mr. Tom," Raquel called as she came tripping toward him holding out her hand. "You aren't still mad at me, are you?"

Tom hesitated. He was having a hard time relating this blonde, modish young woman with the fun-loving Indian girl who used to keep the place lively—a hard enough time without trying to remember details.

"Why, honey, I don't remember ever being mad at you."

"Oh, yes, you were once. Don't you remember when I tore down two sides of the corral with the tractor? You were wild before you got it stopped."

"Was I? I remember having to rebuild it. No, I'm not mad. That was a long time ago!"

"Madre de Díos, the devil must have possessed me to do

such a thing! I climbed up on that little Ford tractor—Daddy had left it running to go get a drink of water—and I wound the fence wire all up in the wheels. I wasn't even scared."

She slanted her blue eyes up at him. What a girl she had become!

They wouldn't stay in the house with the Wilsons. They insisted on camping out in their old quarters in the hay barn, their Texas home. The crucifix and little statue of the Virgin were still over the door where they'd left them to watch over and protect the Wilson family.

"I never pass those symbols," Tom told me, although the Wilsons were not Catholics, "without saying a silent prayer for the goodness of the Lord for blessing the earth with such people as this humble Mayan and his family.

"That's one group of wetbacks who didn't slide into migrancy."

Little New Girl Citizens

MARCH 17, 1970. THE DAY WAS COOL AND blustery. A norther with tornado overtones was on its way toward us, according to the radio. Lee and I were taking our siesta. The patio bell rang hard. Lee went to the door.

"Carrol, you are wanted," she called.

Matías was at the door with his two slender, pretty little girls, six and eight. Each was dressed in her best dress, shining orange shoes, a white pinafore, as if for communion. Their faces were radiant and their eyes sparkling. Matías's face was suffused with proud pleasure; a wide grin revealed a missing side tooth.

Each girl clutched a long white business envelope. They had driven all the way from their lawyer's office in McAllen to show me the contents, for each white envelope contained a paper that said its owner was now a full-fledged United States citizen. They could walk and ride where they pleased over here. They could go to school.

It was the culmination of a long, tortuous, expensive road that Matías traveled to get his little family naturalized. I won't attempt to give an account of all the difficult steps along the way; I don't even know them all. In the end, it hinged on Matías being able to prove to the court that he had spent as much time each year, for a certain number of years, in residence in this country, as he claimed he had.

He came to me to help him find proof. I had nothing. After Hurricane Beulah went through here, we found many things soaked and ruined, many other things that needed drying out, and we got no drying-out weather. Long green mold formed. When the house was dry enough later to camp in, it needed repairing: a new roof, new windows, new siding. We simply carried things out to the incinerator—we had no place to put them, and many were of doubtful value. Most of my old farm accounts, check stubs, and government farm papers went. When former wetbacks came, needing information, I had little left with which to help them.

Lee's two dresser drawers full of snapshots and negatives were among the few things that were not soaked by Beulah. She spent innumerable hours going through and sorting these, dividing them into boxes, one for each of our seven children. Among them she found a picture of about thirty Mexicans standing outside our house, with some of our children in it as well. Lee put it to one side. When some of the men came by later for a visit, I showed them the picture. They enjoyed locating themselves in the picture—and there was Matías, a boy then in 1947.

Each year when the men had gone home after picking cotton, Lee had taken a picture of the group with her old red Kodak. I had given each man a print at the time, but the pictures weren't durable, and in the flimsy houses of the poor people over there they hadn't lasted long.

When Matías's lawyer needed proof of Matías's presence here in years past, we fished out this stained little picture and a bunch of old negatives of which we no longer had prints. Lee chose six or eight shots of the men at the end of different seasons and had prints made. After careful searching, Matías found himself in several of these.

I don't know what the legal requirement was, but the pictures were enough to satisfy the judge two months ago that Matías had really been here when he had said.

They are a very happy family. The lawyer told me over the telephone that they were speechless with joy when they left him. By the time they got here, they weren't exactly speechless any more. I really didn't deserve the thanks; Lee did, for she had saved the pictures, and she took the trouble to find the old negatives and have prints made.

The lawyer said that pictures are the best evidence there is.

goats hair vine